THE SUPERHERO GOSPELS

Karen and Roger,

Ever Upward

THE SUPERHERO GOSPELS
© 2017. Jason Korsiak

This is a book of crititcal essays based on motion pictures and isn't authorized by any studio or production company. These essays are the opinion of the author and make no assumptions about the spirituality or the intent of the filmmakers involved with the movies addressed herein.

Portions of this book contain the recounting of personal experiences. The author has attempted to accurately recollect events to the best of his ability and has intentionally altered the names and characteristics of certain persons out of respect for their privacy.

Scripture quotations taken from the Holy Bible, New International Version®, NIV®. Copyright ©1973, 1978, 1984, 2011 by Biblica, Inc.™ Used by permission of Zondervan. All rights reserved worldwide. www.zondervan.com The "NIV" and "New International Version" are trademarks registered in the United States Patent and Trademark Office by Biblica, Inc.™

ISBN-13: 978-1546751069
ISBN-10: 1546751068

Edited by Jason Korsiak and Brian Trumble.
Photography and cover design by Brian Trumble.
Rear cover by Jason Korsiak.

This work is dedicated to my dad – the man who introduced me to superheroes and spent many a Saturday afternoon with me at the comic book store, showing me the best stories that the industry had to offer and supportively listening to me tell him about the stories I wanted to tell, myself.

In Memory of Adam West
(1928 – 2017)
Thank you for bringing a little light
to the Dark Knight.

~ CONTENTS ~

"A hero is an ordinary individual who finds the strength to persevere and endure in spite of overwhelming odds."

Christopher Reeve, *Still Me* (1999)

THE SUPERHERO GOSPELS

Jason Korsiak

~ AN ~
INTRODUCTION

If you could have any superpower,
what would it be?

Would you fly like Superman if you could? Would you prefer to be invisible like Sue Storm from the Fantastic Four? Perhaps, like Mystique from *X-Men*, you wish that you could turn into someone else entirely? Maybe you want to be faster like the Flash or stronger like the Incredible Hulk. Maybe you'd control people's minds like Professor Xavier, or just move objects with it like Jean Grey. Perhaps you would like to teleport, or stop time for a second or two to catch a breath. We all have something special - something *super* - that we wish we could do, and that superpower reveals a lot about us. For example, if you wish you could fly, it might mean you feel tied down or trapped. A desire to be invisible indicates that you feel exposed or insecure. What does the power you wish you had say about you?

Superheroes and their sundry powers are bigger than ever. Four of the ten top-grossing movies of 2016 were based on comic book characters, and that trend doesn't show any sign of slowing down. Critics keep trying to say that we are getting tired of them, but the box office disagrees. Another set of numbers that disagree is whether or not comic book sales improve as a result of the movies. Some report that the films give specific titles a boost, but other reports show that sales figures even out by the end of the year and that there's no lasting impact.[1] Diamond, the biggest comics distributor, reports that the Top 300 titles between all major publishers only sold 89 million copies in 2016.[2] Consider the billions generated by comic book movies, and it suggests to me that audiences are enthusiastic about comic book characters, just not the comic book medium.

As I think about the gargantuan disconnect between comic book sales and the success of comic book movies, it compels me to contemplate the current state of the Church. Depending on what stats you read, 70% of Americans claim that they're Christian, but church attendance does not back that up. Most reconcile the disparity by saying the polls are skewed or that most of the people professing to be Christian really aren't, but I hold a more optimistic position. The bare minimum requirement for Christians is believing that Jesus Christ is Lord and that He was raised from the dead by God (Romans 10:9). All who believe that, Paul says, are saved. All. I can imagine 70% of Americas believing those two things, even if they don't act on those beliefs by attending a church, just as I think that someone can truly love Spider-Man even though they've never read a comic book.

The fact that people will spend $10 or more for the experience of sitting through a 2-hour superhero movie but will not shill out a mere 3 or 4 bucks for a comic that they can read and enjoy forever tells me that the hunger is there for the characters and their adventures. Similarly, I believe society is hungry for the gospel, just not packaged in the ways we are accustomed to. The problem is that without the comic book source material there would be no comic book movies, just as without the bible there would be no gospel message to proclaim.

To connect with outsiders, and to explain things to believers who weren't spiritually mature, Jesus used fictional stories called parables to illuminate the true stories of men and women of the bible. Superheroes are modern parables; fables, with lessons to learn from and morals to draw from. In this book, we'll do just that and explore spiritual themes in 25 superhero movies. Every chapter has a recommended scripture reading and journal questions. I suggest watching the films first, as the reflections are spoiler-heavy, but each includes enough of a plot summary should you choose not to watch them. You will also find rating information to help you discern if the content is appropriate for your taste, but most of the movies we will be examining are PG-13.

In the beginning of this Introduction, I asked what power you would have if you had a choice. Here's the thing, though; most superheroes don't get a choice. They make the most of their circumstances. Peter Parker didn't go looking to be bitten by a radioactive spider any more than Bruce Banner wanted to be hit with the gamma bomb that turned him into the Hulk. A better question would be, *if you were going to be a superhero, who would you become based on the powers you already have?* As we take this journey, I hope you find strength through these heroes to discover the hero God put within you, and inspiration to do for Him what comic book publishers struggle to achieve with their movies: point people back to the source material.

~ 1 ~
SUPERMAN

"They can be a great people, Kal-El, if they wish to be. They only lack the light to show the way. For this reason above all, their capacity for good, I have sent them you ... my only son."

Year: 1978
Distributor: Warner Bros.
Producer: Pierre Spengler
Director: Richard Donner
Writers: Mario Puzu, David Newman, Leslie Newman, and Robert Benton
Runtime: 143 minutes
Rating: PG for peril, some mild sensuality and language

Scripture Reading: Psalm 46

Some of the earliest words of this film set the tone for the kind of movie we're about to see: "This is no fantasy, no careless product of wild imagination." It is clear from the outset that the makers of *Superman* had a goal in mind: to legitimize the superhero genre. I think that the film's legacy speaks for itself that they succeeded.

We open on a cold, white Krypton, a snowy place of

metal and crystals. As if comic movies themselves were on trial, the first characters we see are three criminals in a court hearing conducted by Jor-El, whose calculations predict that their planet is about to explode. Forbidden from leaving the planet himself, he dramatically sends his son to Earth in a craft that looks like a Christmas ornament, saying the world will need his light to guide them to their potential. The baby is found by a kindly old farm couple named the Kents who name him Clark and raise him as their own.

After his earthly father dies from a heart attack, 18–year-old Clark finds a crystal from his ship's wreckage that guides him north. There, he spends the next 12 years in a fortress of solitude learning from a hologram of Jor-el until he's ready to fly on his own. Clark returns, taking a job at a great metropolitan newspaper called the Daily Planet, where he falls in love with Lois Lane. She's in peril by the schemes of Lex Luthor, the self-professed "greatest criminal mind of our time," who plans to blow up the San Andreas fault and sell the remaining land as "beach-front" property.

Superman not only proved superhero films could be both serious and profitable, but also established many of the tropes that we still see in comic adaptations; the wise father figure, parental death, appearances from the actors of prior versions, having the press name the hero, saying a silly line from the comic in an ironic way (the Fortress of Solitude, in this instance), and heroic montages all became genre staples and remain so.

One of my happiest memories is the day my parents took me to Manhattan when I was 6. I had never been to a big city before, and I was overwhelmed. My father serviced copier equipment, and one of his customers was the New York Daily News building on East 42nd, the location used for the Daily Planet. Imagine my joy to see those offices when my dad took me there! He even showed me the intersection where Superman drills into the sewer to find Luthor's lair. It made the movie so much more real. The tagline of the film was "You will believe a man can fly," and I believed it whole-heartedly. The most iconic moment of Superman flying is when Lois Lane hangs from an out-of-control helicopter on the roof of the Daily Planet. She plummets, but Superman meets her halfway and assures her he's got her. "You've got me?" she retorts, "Who's got you?"

Psalm 46 describes God as an ever-present help in the midst of calamity. Reading about the Earth giving way or of roaring waters reminds me of the scenes in the movie where Superman soars to the rescue during the aftermath of Lex's missiles. I think of the times He has held me up, like when Superman protected the train from crashing. The climax, in which Superman reverses time to save Lois, seems like a cop-out to some but illustrates how *our* hero stepped into time just to save us, and the lengths He'd go to do so. After time goes back to normal and Lois is saved, she complains to him about her car, not realizing what her savior went through. I wonder how often we complain to the Lord, unaware of the unseen things He's done to help us?

There are those who find Superman hard to relate to because he's 'too' good, but I submit that we're not *supposed* to relate to Superman; Lois Lane is the one we have more in common with. Like Lois, we can be head-strong and proud. Like Lois, we have a habit of getting into trouble. Like Lois, we have a savior who swoops in no matter how often we get ourselves tied to the railroad tracks.

When you are hanging from the edge, who's got *you?* Fortunately, God's love – like Superman – is bulletproof.

JOURNAL QUESTIONS

- Do you rely more on your own effort or on God's grace?
- Do you think that people recognize God in you? How so?

~ 2 ~
BATMAN

"It's not exactly a normal world, is it?"

Year: 1989
Distributor: Warner Bros.
Producers: John Peters, Peter Guber
Director: Tim Burton
Writers: Sam Hamm and Warren Skaaren
Runtime: 126 minutes
Rating: PG-13

Scripture Reading: 1 Samuel 16:1-13

It was Summer, 1989: Bat-fever was in the air and I'd caught it. I was mesmerized by a full-page ad in our paper, a painting of the Dark Knight swinging through Gotham. My exposure to Batman up to that point had only been Adam West and cartoons like *Super Friends*. That painting told me that I was in for something different, and the film's opening fanfare indicated what a monumental experience I was about to have. It felt like a rite of passage, like every other iteration was for kids but now, at 6 years old, I was a man because I watched the grownup version and saw the *real* Batman.

I had a chance to watch it again the October prior to this writing at a theater showing classic movies for the fall. I wasn't alone in my journey to Gotham, though; a couple of friends joined me. One of them was a young woman in her 20s who'd never seen *any* Batman movie and knew very little about him, so I was particularly curious about what she'd think of it. Admittedly, she isn't a moviegoer and chalks her inability to sit through them up to her ADHD. In fact, she insists that the movie was 6 ½ hours long, despite saying she liked it. The best part of seeing it with her was when Joker pulls a comically long revolver from his trousers and downs the Batwing with a single shot.

"What," she said flatly. Then, as the Batwing crashed, she casually added, "Yeah, no."

She also demystified Joker's makeup, pointing out the times when you could see Jack's real lips under the latex ones. I was startled by her laughter when Bruce announces himself to Vicki and Knox in the armory. As they discuss a weird-looking suit of armor, Bruce appears and says that it's Japanese. When Knox asks why he thinks that, he replies, "Because I bought it in Japan." It was funnier to my friend because, like Knox and Vicki, she was meeting Bruce Wayne for the first time too.

Part of what makes this joke (and Keaton) effective is that he appears so unassuming. You wouldn't think that he spends his nights skulking in alleys wearing a batsuit. That's what director Tim Burton wanted. It's widely known that the casting of Michael Keaton was met with fan resistance, who feared that having "Mr. Mom" as Batman hinted at another silly rendition of the character. Batman is tall and chiseled in the comics; Burton's position was that a big guy wouldn't need a costume to look intimidating, but a man of Keaton's frame would. Contrasting Keaton is Nicholson as the larger-than-life Joker. The Joker's self-worshipping plan is to make everyone look like him by poisoning cosmetics, which will kill them in the process. When that fails, he throws a parade to poison them with gas in the streets.

A similarly unlikely casting choice is made in today's scripture, in which the prophet Samuel anoints a new king. God warns Samuel not to look for someone of stature. Like Burton casting Batman, God looked for inward strength, not outward appearance. Slight and modest, David was as perfect for the role of king as Keaton was for Batman. Comic fans still complain about casting decisions, and we in the church can likewise judge others by appearances. We even hide our true selves. Sometimes we do this because of sin, but more often it's the fear that our faith will be questioned if we let others see we're not okay. Like Keaton trying to bulk up, we wear spiritual batsuits to seem tougher. At the other extreme, we can be like the Joker and throw our brokenness a parade and invite others to join in our misery.

Like the Pharisees, who were also afraid of appearing spiritually deficient, our faces can be as whitewashed as the Joker's and our smiles as fake as his rubber grin (Matthew 23:27-28). Someone will eventually see the real us behind the facade, though, just like my friend spotted Nicholson's real lips. God searches hearts like Vicki Vale investigating Bruce Wayne; He sees the roses we lay in the street to honor our pain. 1 Peter 3:3-4 says that the best adorning we can wear is the gentle spirit of our true heart. It might mean appearing weak, but God is strong in weakness (1 Corinthians 12:10). Free of the burden of appearances, we can turn our focus to helping the hurting, putting on something stronger than a batsuit – *compassion*.

JOURNAL QUESTIONS
- Have you ever felt judged for your emotions?
- How can we be more aware of other people's feelings?

~ 3 ~
SPIDER-MAN

"Remember, with great power comes great responsibility."

Year: 2002
Distributor: Columbia Pictures
Producers: Laura Ziski, Ian Bryce
Director: Sam Raimi
Writer: David Koepp
Runtime: 121 minutes
Rating: PG-13 for stylized violence and action

Scripture Reading: Matthew 25:14-30

I have an embarrassing confession to make. I was so excited for the release of today's film that I saw it in theaters *nine* times when it came out in May 2002. Furthermore, the film was the basis for the second sermon I ever gave, but more on that later. *Spider-Man* is the story of Peter Parker, who, bitten by a genetically-altered super spider, develops the proportionate agility and strength of a spider, as well as its abilities to spin webs and climb walls. In addition to all of these amazing gifts, Peter also gains a heightened sense that alerts him of danger. This comes in handy as he embarks on his quest of becoming an underground cage fighter.

Yes, "Puny" Parker, who has been pushed around his entire life, sees his newfound powers as a way of showing off to the girl he likes, Mary Jane Watson. In the comics, MJ doesn't fully appear until *Amazing Spider-Man #42*, having been teased for months. Here, MJ is "the girl next door," whom Peter has had a crush on since grade school. Another divergence that the film makes from Spidey's origin comic is how long he was a wrestler. Peter fights only one match in the film but is a wrestling superstar in the comic, appearing on late night talk shows and becoming a household name.

One thing the movie does have in common with the comic, however, is that Peter is an orphan raised by his Aunt May and Uncle Ben. While the film has Uncle Ben deliver the well-trod *Spider-Man* quote about great power and great responsibility, the comic is much more dramatic. Puffed up, Peter decides not to stop a robber who runs past him after one of his fights. Later, he goes home to a distraught Aunt May and discovers that they have been robbed and that Ben is dead. Outraged, he hunts down the thief only to discover that it's the robber he didn't stop when he had the chance. The comic, *Amazing Fantasy #15*, concludes with Peter shrinking into the shadows, his head hung in shame. The narration, by Spider-Man co-creator Stan Lee, reads, "And a lean, silent figure slowly fades into the gathering darkness, aware at last that in this world with great power there must also come – great responsibility."[1]

The first lesson I ever gave was on a youth ski trip and was inspired by Freddy Krueger. The following year, I did one on Spider-Man. The youth pastor was so impressed that he asked me to deliver it as a sermon. Since then, it's become my signature message. Articulating spiritual truths from pop culture is one of my talents, but we all have them, and each is a gift from God (1 Corinthians 12:4-11).

Our understanding of talents is largely informed by today's reading, a parable about a rich man about to go on a long trip. Before he leaves, he divides his wealth amongst three servants. A 'talent' was a unit of money worth seven years of wages. When he returned, two of his servants had doubled the talents he gave them, but the servant who only received one talent hid it out of fear. Angry that his servant wasted the opportunity, he took the talent back and threw him out in the street. There, a lean, silent figure slowly faded into the gathering darkness, aware at last that in this world with great power there must also come great responsibility.

Like Peter becoming a wrestler, we can be tempted to use our talents for ourselves. There is no sin in making your living from your talents, but God gives them to us for much more. 1 Peter 4:10 states, "Each of you should use whatever gift you have received to serve others, as faithful stewards of God's grace in its various forms." Stewardship means that we have to give it back at some point, and, like the rich man in the story, God expects interest. So, use what He's given you to the full; you might discover additional abilities you didn't even know you had.

Many of us are like the servant who buried his talent, not recognizing the treasure we have or how capable we are to utilize it. Your talents aren't random; God would not give them to you if you were unqualified. You have great power, even if you do not realize it, and the tingle you feel that you let hold you back isn't a spider sense warning you of danger; it's the Lord telling you to swing into action.

JOURNAL QUESTIONS
- What are your talents? How can you used them to serve?
- How can thinking of our talents as gifts from God help to compel them to use them?

~ 4 ~
FANTASTIC FOUR

"Am I the only one who thinks this is cool?"

Year: 2005
Distributor: 20th Century Fox
Producers: Avi Arad, Bernd Eichinger, Ralph Winter
Director: Tim Story
Writers: Mark Frost and Michael France
Runtime: 106 minutes
Rating: PG-13 for sequences of intense action, and some suggestive content

Scripture Reading: Ecclesiastes 12:9-13

Today's film has an unfortunate reputation as a bad movie, scoring 27% on *Rotten Tomatoes.* It made only $154 million against its $100 million at the US box office, which, though enough to warrant a sequel, is not exactly impressive. Response was mixed to negative, with a census among critics that the movie was mediocre.

The history of this film's production is as unusual as the finished product is disappointing. *Fantastic Four* was originally made for $1 million by Roger Corman, the king of B-movie schlock, in an attempt for license holder Bernd Eichinger to maintain the film rights, produced without any intention of releasing it.[1] The film is available on YouTube as if this writing, so give it a watch; it's a lot of fun and better represents the characters than the big screen versions.

Marvel bought back the film rights and sold them to Fox, who spent a better part of the 90's trying to get a movie together, frequently changing writers and directors. As with the Corman version, it became another race against time to make a film so that the rights could be held onto. After this film and its sequel did poorly, Fox threw together *another* version in 2015 for the sole purpose of *(again)* holding onto the rights. It's sad; everyone wants the Fantastic Four, but no one knows what to do with them.

The finished product is a directionless slog that loses momentum after the first act, which, in all fairness, does an excellent job of establishing the characters, getting them into space, setting up the villain, and giving them their powers by the 30 minute mark. The tone is light, and most of the cast feel like their comic book counterparts, especially Michael Chiklis as the Thing and Chris Evans as the Human Torch. Their banter is perfect, and Evans is so spot-on I'm certain he could play both Human Torch *and* Captain America in the same movie and I'd think they were different people. Where the casting fizzles is Julian McMahon as Victor. He's less like Doctor Doom and more like Willem Defoe as the Green Goblin in *Spider-Man*, complete with a cornball mask and a Board of Directors he murders after they give him the boot from his own company.

Fantastic Four wastes its second act having the heroes squabble in a lab trying to figure out how to get rid of their powers, culminating with a rushed climax about corporate revenge. It's a far cry from the sci fi adventures imagined by comics creators Stan Lee and Jack Kirby. Why is it so hard to translate the Fantastic Four to the screen?

The Teacher in Ecclesiastes says we complicate things with too many books; the more versions of something we make, the more we distance it from its original essence. Fox definitely did that with *Fantastic Four*, but we do it with the bible too. We stretch, like Reed Richards, and reach beyond orthodoxy and exchange it for trends. We wrap force field bubbles around ourselves like Sue Storm to shield ourselves from contradiction, then get fired up like the Human Torch if somebody comes close to popping them. Our foundation stops being the Rock of Ages and becomes a craggy thing, chiseled by pundits and talking heads. Instead of immersing ourselves in the Word, we read only books *about* it, looking for theologies that suit us. Obviously, there's nothing wrong with reading spiritual books (I'd be a hypocrite if I said that in a book such as this), but our studies should point us back to scripture, not act as a substitute for it.

Christianity like that is not about Jesus; it's a *brand,* entwined with such things as political affiliation or fads in Christian media. Simply believing in Jesus as the risen Lord is what makes you a Christian. Not your clothes. Not your taste in music. Not how you vote. Conversely, those things don't keep you from being a Christian either.

Just as the studios care more about holding onto the Fantastic Four's film rights than making a good movie, the pundits will continue to muddle our faith to hold onto you. But in my experience, nonbelievers don't dislike Jesus; they are put off by that added baggage. Luckily, we don't have to add a thing to the gospel; Jesus is enough. In fact, He's more than enough – He's fantastic.

JOURNAL QUESTIONS
- What do you read more, the bible or books about it?
- How can focusing on others' interpretations of the bible rather than scripture itself be a door to false teaching?

~ 5 ~
X-MEN

"Are you a God-fearing man, Senator? Such a strange phrase. I've always seen God as a teacher. As a bringer of light, wisdom, and understanding. No, I think what you really are afraid of is me. Me and my kind."

Year: 2000
Distributor: 20th Century Fox
Producers: Lauren Shuler Donner, Ralph Winter
Director: Bryan Singer
Writer: David Hayter
Runtime: 104 minutes
Rating: PG-13 for sci fi action violence

Scripture Reading: Matthew 5:43-48

After a decade of *Batman* sequels, each progressively worse than the last, as well as failed attempts to launch new franchises like *Steel* and *Spawn*, 2000's *X-Men* reinvigorated faith in both superhero movies as well as Marvel Comics. In 1998, Marvel had a hit with *Blade*, but *X-Men* brought the publisher a mainstream success that R-Rated movies such as *Blade* could not. Not until 2016's *Deadpool*, anyway.

X-Men is about a race of people called mutants who live in hiding because they're born with an X gene that gives them special abilities, making normal humans fearful. The movie begins at Auschwitz, reminding us what prejudice can lead to, as a boy named Erik Lensherr watches Nazis take his parents away, awakening his powers over magnetism. Years later, he runs into Professor Charles Xavier, a former ally, at a senate hearing concerning Mutant Registration.

There are three perspectives regarding Mutant Rights; Xavier's, who founded a school where he teaches mutants to defend a world that fears and hates them; Magneto's, who thinks that no harmony is possible and that mutants must replace humans before they are put in chains; and Senator Kelly's, who campaigns for Registration because he fears that giving mutants rights will impinge his own. As it happens, these men also represent three points of view in the Church.

Kelly's desire to regulate how others live is not unlike those who support legislating from the pulpit. For them, it stands to reason that if our morals are correct, then everyone should live by them. But forcing nonbelievers to live by our standards does not save them, it only perpetuates the lie that 'being a good person' is enough to get into heaven. Our goal should be changing hearts, not lifestyles.

This brings us to Magneto, whose radical solution is unleashing a machine on a summit of world leaders that will turn them into mutants so they'll become sympathetic to his cause. His first test is on Kelly. Rather than doing the hard work of persuading others, he plans to force conversion, not unlike medieval Inquisitors who used machines of torture to pressure converts. Modern Magnetos don't have conversion machines but manipulate people using tools like guilt and fear. Such efforts do more harm and, just as Kelly dies as a result of Magneto's efforts, don't usually stick.

In today's passage, Jesus says to love our persecutors and show mercy to our enemies. This is also Xavier's stance, who founded the X-Men on that principle. Paul expands on Jesus' directive in Romans 12:20, in which he tells us to feed and clothe our enemies; doing so heaps "burning coals onto their heads." A strange phrase, it means *to purify*. We turn enemies into brothers, not by force but by kindness.

Magneto appears to understand this when talking to Kelly, saying that he thinks of God as a bringer of light, wisdom, and understanding. Specifically, he pictures God as a teacher. Magneto's image of God is *Professor Xavier;* yet, rather than following Xavier's teachings, Magneto proceeds with his plan, proving Kelly right that mutants are a threat.

How often do *our* actions confirm others' disbelief? 1 Peter 2:12 instructs believers to live honorably so that our antagonists have no choice but to glorify God. In addition, 1 Thessalonians 4:12 teaches that living a quiet life of hard work and minding our business is how we win outsiders. We can prove our persecutors right by responding to their hate with more hate, or we can prove the gospel right by turning the other cheek and showing that our way works.

You can be like Kelly and sanction people, you can find brotherhood with fellow Magnetos and force your will on your persecutors, or you can be X-Men. The 'X' doesn't stand for the mutant X gene in our case, though; the letter X comes from Chi, a Greek character used to represent Christ when typefacing was expensive in the early days of print. The best example? Xmas. Some find it offensive, but the 'X' in Xmas literally stands for *Christ.* What do you stand for? Do you stand for humility? For mercy? For loving your enemies? If so, you are an X-Man; Christ's man.

JOURNAL QUESTIONS
- What group do you have the hardest time understanding?
- How can Mutant Registration apply to real life issues?

~ 6 ~
DAREDEVIL

"You didn't come here for forgiveness. You came for permission, and I can't give you that."

Year: 2003
Distributor: 20th Cetury Fox
Producers: Avi Arad, Gary Foster. Arnon Milchan
Director: Mark Steven Johnson
Writer: Mark Steven Johnson
Runtime: 93 minutes
Rating: PG-13 for action/violence and some sensuality

Scripture Reading: Isaiah 1:17

Serving as Ben Affleck's demo reel for *Batman V. Superman*, *Daredevil* is the story of a blind man with superhuman senses who fearlessly roves the streets in a search for justice following the killing of his father. Though he is Daredevil by night, by day Matt Murdock is a struggling lawyer whose firm languishes under his policy of representing only those whom he believes are innocent. Along the way, he falls in love with a woman named Elektra whose father is killed by the same Kingpin of crime that murdered his.

Daredevil is inconsistent, with a number of things in its favor but simultaneously bogged down by the clichès that were wearing themselves thin by the time of its release in 2003. Musical segues from bands that are long-since dated, rapid-fire editing, self-indulgent narration, and a dependence on black leather were all earmarks of the time, and they were all winding down. *Daredevil* also suffers for just how much it borrows from other films. The playground scene in which Matt fights Elektra (probably the stupidest part of the film) is straight out of *The Matrix Reloaded*. Various details of the 1989 *Batman* are used: the tenacious reporter character that no one believes, having the villain be the one who killed the hero's parents in spite of it not being that way in the comics, a love interest who wishes the hero would "let her in," laying roses on the street, making a cathedral the setting for the finale, and then dropping the villain to his death from the top of it. They even took the 'hero rejects an invite to a ball but goes anyway because the girl he likes is there' plot device from *Batman Returns*. He back flips away from projectiles like Spider-Man, and his father dies in the street like Uncle Ben. They repeat that trope with Elektra's father, giving us *two* 'dead parents in the street' scenes.

It's unfortunate, as *Daredevil* is strong when it does

its own thing. Small details, like having the credits in braille or giving us insight into Matt's routine as a blind man, help ground the film, and scenes like Matt using his sonar to see Elektra in the rain are touching. The film's greatest strength, however, is showcasing an obsession with justice.

While most vigilante-style heroes like Batman or the Punisher are on a quest for justice, no other hero embodies it better than Matt Murdock, who works as a lawyer in the judicial system in addition to being Daredevil. Justice is all-engrossing for him. Justice is understood differently through various philosophical perspectives, but two forms at work in this film are Judicial and Divine. Matt is a deeply religious man but feels no remorse over killing criminals, because he views it as a correction to legal oversight. A rapist goes free early in the film, for instance, so Daredevil seeks retribution. Countering Matt's perspective is the priest he confesses to, who sees what Matt calls *justice* as *vengeance;* murdering a rapist isn't about equity, it's about anger. Anger is also what drives Elektra to target Daredevil for the death of her father.

In Romans 12:19, Paul stresses the importance of not seeking vengeance but letting the Lord's wrath balance out the injustices that we are dealt. Henry Wadworth Longfellow translated a poem on the topic by German satirist Friedrich von Logau: *"Though the mills of God grind slowly; Yet they grind exceeding small; Though with patience He stands waiting, With exactness grinds He all."* This is a variation on what 2nd Century philosopher Sextus Empericus wrote about the millstones of the gods, that they "grind late, but fine." We want justice on our terms, but not only does God know better, He's better at it. He's the adjudicator, not us. He also sees our secret motives when we try to avenge ourselves.

Today's scripture says to seek justice, to do goodness, and to plead the case of the powerless. The verse is a further reminder of our role in God's court. We're neither judge nor prosecutor. There is a prosecutor, though; he doesn't wear a horned mask or wield a billy club, but he *is* a devil. Jesus is the Defense, and our job is to be His witnesses. That said, we can *seek* justice here on Earth like Matt Murdock, defending those who have been treated unjustly.

JOURNAL QUESTIONS

- Have you ever seen someone 'get what they deserve' for an injustice they did to you? What did you feel?
- Who in your life is in need of mercy and forgiveness?

~ 7 ~
TEENAGE MUTANT NINJA TURTLES

"Together, there is nothing your four minds cannot accomplish. Help each other, draw upon one another, and always remember the power that binds you."

Year: 1990
Distributor: New Line Cinema
Producers: Simon Fields, David Chan, Kim Dawson
Director: Steve Barron
Writers: Todd W. Langen and Bobby Herbeck
Runtime: 93 minutes
Rating: PG

Scripture Reading: Ecclesiastes 4:9-12

Some of you might wonder what this film is doing on our viewing list. Others of you know, of course, that the Ninja Turtles began as a comic book. It was a surprisingly dark and violent comic book, as a matter of fact, and has a tie to another comic book hero – Daredevil. In yesterday's entry, we saw young Matt Murdock get exposed to chemicals that gave him superpowers. The creators of the Ninja Turtles wanted to parody superheroes and wrote that the turtles were transformed by a canister of ooze which hit a young man in the face and then rolled into the sewer. That young man was implied to be Matt Murdock.[1]

Today's movie glosses over that part of the origin but does hark back to the grittier roots of the franchise rather than the colorful palette of the cartoon. We open in a grimy, crime-worn New York where the Foot Clan (a parody of the Hand from, again, *Daredevil*) recruits kids into their gang by offering them a clubhouse that looks like Cobra Kai opened a Chuck E. Cheese on Pleasure Island, complete with all the soda, arcade games, and cigarettes a 10-year-old could want. Presiding over them is Shredder, a Darth Vader analog so on-the-nose that he even apes Anakin Skywalker's famous quote, "I am your father."

Shredder's arch nemesis is a rat named Splinter (who, *again*, is a parody of Stick from *Daredevil*), the surrogate dad and trainer of our eponymous reptiles. Splinter is taken by the Foot, sending Leonardo, Donatello, Michelangelo, and Raphael on a mission to rescue him. They're joined by a TV reporter named April O'Neill and Casey Jones, a vigilante.

The conflict of the film is largely a juxtaposition of two very different "families." One is Splinter and the Turtles;

the other is the Foot, which recruits its young members by exploiting their feelings of disconnect from their parents. Our conduit into the Foot Clan is the son of April's boss, who's run away because he thinks his dad doesn't love him. The dynamic between the turtles is like a smaller version of that dispute, with Raphael acting as the family loner. Raph also gets more development than the other three. Leonardo leads, but at no time does Donatello "do machines," like the cartoon theme song promised. Michelangelo is a party dude, though.

Raph's undoing is his persistent breaking away from the group. Defying Splinter's rules, Raphael goes out of the shadows and into the streets to fight crime by himself. Later on, he is overpowered by the Foot Clan, illustrating today's scripture reading, "Pity anyone who falls and has no one to help them up ... Though one may be overpowered, two can defend themselves." Raph is the one who falls alone.

After Raph is pulverized, the group goes to April's family home in the country where they nurse him to health. Leo never leaves Raph's side until he awakens, reminding me of the Parable of the Good Samaritan, about a man who is robbed and left for dead. Religious leaders and members of his faith ignore him, but a stranger from a rival group has sympathy and helps. Jesus tells the parable after being asked who our neighbors are; neighbors are those who are there for each other.

Splinter prepared the turtles to work as a team when he is gone. Likewise, Jesus established the apostles as a model for how the Church should function. It's tempting to be like Raph and go our own way; other times, we feel alone when we might not be. What we see as *absence* is sometimes just a communication barrier or an inability to utilize our support network. That barrier isn't a wall, it's a mirror showing us a false image that we have no one. This can frustrate us and get us lost in our own heads. Splinter warns Raph that when we turn anger inward, it becomes an unconquerable enemy. This enemy dulls us, which is why teamwork is so critical; as iron sharpens iron, Proverbs 27:17 says, teamwork motivates us to try harder than we might on our own. If you do not have that camaraderie, seek it. Finding fellow turtles might feel daunting, but all it takes is stepping out of your shell.

JOURNAL QUESTIONS
- Who is your support network?
- How can we be more intentional about relying on others?

~ 8 ~
THE INCREDIBLES

"And when everyone's super, no one will be."

Year: 2004
Distributor: Buena Vista Pictures
Producer: John Walker
Director: Brad Bird
Writer: Brad Bird
Runtime: 115 minutes
Rating: PG-13 for action violence.

Scripture Reading: 1 John 2:18-19, 4:1-3

An example of what a Fantastic Four movie *should* be, Pixar's superhero opus is about a world where "Supers" have gone into hiding because the public started suing them over their acts of derring-do. Former hero Mr. Incredible is having a mid-life crisis, and his longing for the glory days draws him into the trap of Syndrome, a villain whose plan is to threaten a city with a killer robot but pose as a new hero by stopping it. He just has to make sure that no Supers are left to get in his way.

I compare it to the Fantastic Four because, well, just look at the lineup: Violet is invisible and can project force fields, Elastigirl can stretch, Mr. Incredible is a Thing-like strongman with a heart of gold, and his son Jack-Jack can burst into flames (among other things). Elastigirl and Mr. Incredible have another son, Dash, with speed powers that better represent velocity than most movies with supersonic characters. Usually, they're an indecipherable blur or slowed down in bullet-time. Dash is just fast; his limbs move at lightning speeds. It's also a better Fantastic Four movie in that the team faces larger than life threats (such as the Mole Man-inspired Underminer), has fun doing it, *and* manages to be a thoughtful look at the pitfalls of superhero family life. Moreover, *The Incredibles* is a great lens through which to examine the dangers of false prophets.

Thanks to the Incredibles, Syndrome doesn't do a lot of damage as a false hero, being defeated quickly by his own infernal machine and then by an infant. False prophets, on the other hand, can be a bit harder to contend with. Today's passage alerts us that, while there's an Antichrist coming, the world is already filled with them. We need to test spiritual leaders and their teachings to assure that they are from God.

Matthew 24:24 also discusses false prophets, warning

that they will perform miracles to undermine believers. Such false prophets, it says in Romans 16:18, don't serve the Lord but themselves. Smooth-talkers, they are able to deceive the spiritually immature. Most ministers aren't false teachers, of course, but false teachers cast a pall over Christianity, and make ministering to the unchurched much harder.

Syndrome's objective is to make everyone super. One could argue that there is a kernel of nobility to this goal. In the same way, a good pastor can lose direction with the best of intentions. Challenging them does more than defend the gospel, it offers them the chance to be restored. They need to be receptive, however. A deep sense of conviction can harden a pastor's resolve as much as it inspires others to join it.

That charisma is one reason a false prophet rises to power. People gravitate towards preachers who say what they want to hear and sound confident while saying it. There isn't anything wrong with looking for a church where you fit in or where the lessons apply to you, but it becomes a problem when that means looking for a pastor whose sermons don't invite introspection. A pastor should be like Edna Mode, the quirky fashion designer who makes costumes for Supers. She is supportive, but loves you enough to slap you back to your senses when you get off track.

The only way to test the spirits of your teachers is by knowing what the bible says. The task might seem daunting, but, to continue our discussion from the last chapter, this is another reason why it's important to be in connection with others. Mr. Incredible admits that he isn't strong enough to defeat Syndrome. Elastigirl tells him that working together means he doesn't have to be. Similarly, it's easier to expose false teachings when we pool our knowledge.

There are Syndromes out there who scratch the itchy ears of judgment, growing personality cults under a flag of prejudice rather than the cross of mercy. Others exploit the poor, offering promises of abundance while filling their own pockets. Edna Mode says luck favors the prepared; to defeat the heresies of life's Syndromes, we must prepare by joining with other spiritual Supers and by studying scripture. That said, luck favors the prepared, but God favors the humble.

JOURNAL QUESTIONS
- What do you look for in a church? Does it challenge you?
- Are you in a bible study? If not, who can you join with?

~ 9 ~
GHOST RIDER

"He may have my soul, but he doesn't have my spirit."

Year: 2007
Distributor: 20th Cetury Fox
Producers: Avi Arad, Steven Paul, Michael De Luca, Gary Foster
Director: Mark Steven Johnson
Writer: Mark Steven Johnson
Runtime: 114 minutes
Rating: PG-13 for horror violence and disturbing images

Scripture Reading: 1 Thessalonians 5:23-24

Stunt rider Johnny Blaze sells his soul to the devil, as played by Peter Fonda, in exchange for curing his father's cancer. The cost is a curse which turns Blaze into a demonic bounty hunter on a mission to defeat the devil's upstart son, Blackheart, who's come in search of a soul contract that will let him bring hell to Earth and rule it, overthrowing Fonda. Conflicted, Blaze tries to control his curse on a quest for redemption while rediscovering the woman he loves, whom he left as a young man because of his affliction.

Nicolas Cage is a famously passionate fan of comics. He was set to play Superman in a Tim Burton reboot which was never made, named his son Kal-El based on Superman's true name, and even has a tattoo of Ghost Rider which had to be covered up so that he could *play* Ghost Rider. Cage is also one of the things that keep the movie from greatness. When in Rider form, Cage is clearly having a blast. Every second that the Rider is on screen is gold. Yet, when he's in his human form as Johnny Blaze, Cage's performance feels disjointed and inconsistent, relying too heavily on *quirks* (such as 'drinking' jelly beans from a martini glass). Villain Blackheart is the biggest issue with the film, who is generic and symptomatic of when the film was made. In the comics, Blackheart is a giant shadow monster with a mane of spines and a whipping tail. Here, he's a wispy, bleach-skinned pretty boy in a black coat who occasionally does that "demon face" warp that used to be all the rage on YouTube.

Weak villain and erratic hero aside, *Ghost Rider* is an improvement over writer/director Mark Steven Johnson's earlier effort, *Daredevil.* The chemistry between the leads is more convincing, and there's less reliance on choppy edits or musical segues. Balancing werewolf-like horror themes with superheroes and religious allegory in a movie that feels like a western could not have been easy, but it's well-balanced and has several fun moments. When it's not trying too hard to be funny, the film is surprisingly philosophical and with a single line (this chapter's epigraph) elucidates that our soul and our spirit aren't the same thing.

C.S. Lewis is often misquoted as saying that we don't have souls but that we *are* souls and *have* bodies. The quote is actually a paraphrase of an 1881 paper by a Rev. Dr. R. Thornton, whose position is categorically un-Christian and is steeped in Gnosticism, the heresy which taught that our spiritual and physical selves are distinct and that what we do with one does not affect the other. We can sin all we want, Gnostics said, because our souls are saved. This contradicts what it says in Romans 6:2, "Shall we go on sinning so that grace may increase? By no means! We are those who have died to sin; how can we live in it any longer?" It could be argued that we do not lose our salvation over the sins in our life, but that doesn't mean our actions aren't important or that they don't have consequences.

Humans aren't just body and soul; we are body, soul, and spirit; a trinity unto ourselves. Today's scripture makes a distinction between these separate components of our being, and Hebrews 4:12 defines their interplay as being like bones marrow. Marrow fills our bones, without it they dry up. Our souls, similarly, wither without the Holy Spirit.

1 Corinthians 6:19 says that our bodies are temples for God, bought for the price paid on the cross. God owns our souls, but not all of us let Him take up residence. A lot of people out there are 'empty churches,' occupied by evil instead of being alive in Christ (Ephesians 2:5). This is why the word we use for them is *condemned;* these 'buildings' are not going to last.

My grandfather had a saying to summarize the other extreme: "too heavenly minded to be earthly good." We can be too spiritual at the expense of our humanity. Just as the Trinity is One God who is Father, Son, and Spirit, we're one person who is body, spirit, and soul – and we should invest accordingly. If *Ghost Rider* can balance superheroes, horror, and westerns, surely we can find balance within ourselves.

JOURNAL QUESTIONS
- Which of the three aspects do you invest the most into?
- How can enrich all three and find unity between them?

~ 10 ~
HELLBOY

"He was born a demon; we can't change that.
But you will help him, in essence, to
become a man."

Year: 2004
Distributor: Columbia Pictures
Producers: Lawrence Gordon, Mike Richardson, Lloyd Levin
Director: Guillermo Del Toro
Writer: Guillermo Del Toro
Runtime: 122 minutes
Rating: PG-13 for sci-fi action violence and frightening images

Scripture Reading: Mark 14:3-9

John Hurt, who plays Professor Broom, passed away just days before writing today's entry. In watching the film again, I was all the more touched by his death and funeral scenes. Hurt brings warmth and repose to the character of Broom, a paranormal expert who raises a demon as his son. Towards the end of his life, the diabolical force that brought Hellboy into this world returns to finish what he started.

The movie begins during World War II. Nazis have recruited Rasputin to open a portal to a place where ancient, Lovecraftian gods slumber, but allied forces find and close it. Rasputin is pulled in as it collapses, but not before an infant demon escapes. Broom catches the baby, naming him Hellboy. Together with other 'freaks,' like a psychic fish-man, they live in a waste treatment facility that acts as a front for the Bureau of Paranormal Research and Defense, a shadowy organization that fights supernatural threats. The story picks up in the present, with Broom discovering that he is dying. He sends for an FBI agent named Myers to act as Hellboy's new caretaker.

In spite of his demonic heritage, Broom has always treated Hellboy as his son. Hellboy is immature, more like a teenager who just wants to fit in. He even grinds his horns to stumps to seem more human, not that it matters; he's all but a prisoner at the Bureau but escapes now and then to see the woman he loves, a tortured pyrokinetic named Liz.

Rasputin is brought back from the dead. His plan is to use Hellboy to reopen the portal and bring about the end of the world, a new order ruled by tentacled horrors in the sky. He infiltrates the Bureau and has his top assassin kill Broom, leaving an evidence trail to guide Hellboy to him.

To raise the stakes, Rasputin steals Liz's soul, sending it to the realm of the aforementioned gods, which look like tentacled space whales. Blinded by his love for Liz, Hellboy starts to open the portal, but Myers snaps him out of it by holding up Broom's rosary. Rasputin convinced Hellboy he was an irredeemable demon, but Myers' act reminded him that his father's love made him more.

After defeating Rasputin once and for all and closing the portal, Hellboy whispers into Liz's ear, resuscitating her. Liz asks Hellboy what he said, so he tells her. "Hey you, on the other side. Let her go, because for her I will cross over. And then you'll be sorry."

It's funny how a devil can be a metaphor for what Jesus did for us. Unlike Hellboy, Jesus didn't just threaten; He descended into death (Ephesians 4:9), proclaimed to the dead (1 Peter 3:19), set the captives free (Ephesians 4:8), and holds to the keys to death and hell (Revelation 1:18). Jesus' preeminence allows us to be adopted into His family like Broom adopted Hellboy. We don't have horns or a tail, but we all start out as equally on the wrong side of the fence and are equally able to be redeemed.

The movie ends with a question, "What makes a man a man ... is it his origins, the way he came to life? I don't think so. It's the choices he makes. Not how he starts things but how he decides to end them."

A woman of similarly disreputable origins makes a bold, life-changing choice in today's passage, anointing Jesus' feet with perfume and then drying them with her hair. The story is in all four gospels but with minor variations. Luke tells us that she was a repenting sinner, but John adds that she was Mary, sister of Lazarus, whom Jesus raised from the dead. Seeing her brother alive again must have been as faith-affirming to her as seeing Hellboy call Liz back from death was for Myers at the end of the movie. In fact, I've wondered if the miracle wasn't for her benefit to start with.

Just as Hellboy can't change being born a demon, we can't change our beginnings, but we can choose to respond when Jesus calls us out of the tomb of our hearts, and allow God to adopt us. He crossed over for us; all He asks is that we take a step for Him.

JOURNAL QUESTIONS
- Where do you find the greatest sense of belonging?
- What does it mean for you to be "adopted" by God?

~ 11 ~
THE WOLVERINE

"A man can run out of things to live for."

Year: 2013
Distributor: 20th Century Fox
Producers: Donald De Line, Greg Berlanti
Director: James Mangold
Writers: Mark Bomback, Scott Frank
Runtime: 126 minutes
Rating: PG-13 for sequences of intense sci-fi action and violence, some sexuality and language

Scripture Reading: Judges 16:15-22

Based on the beloved 1982 comic book mini-series by Chris Claremont and Frank Miller, *The Wolverine* takes a number cues from the source material but also shoehorns a villain that wasn't there, adds characters, changes others, and forces us to remember *X-Men: The Last Stand* happened by including weird "ghost of Jean Grey" hallucinations.

Logan is tormented by the guilt of having killed Jean Grey and has become a hermit in the hopes of never hurting anyone again. Considering he might live forever because of his healing ability, he will have a long wait. Logan is found and summoned to Japan to say goodbye to a dying soldier named Yashida that he saved in Nagasaki during the nuclear attacks. Yashida has a strange offer; he wants to take Logan's mutant healing ability so that he can live forever. Logan, in turn, would be able to grow old and die, finally ending his pain. Logan declines but finds himself attracted to Yashida's granddaughter, Mariko, who seems to be in danger. The next day, Logan awakens to find Yashida dead, Mariko hunted by ninjas, and that he no longer has his healing factor.

The Wolverine is a well-paced action movie that has the courage to slow down and breathe, something that most modern blockbusters are unwilling to do. Taking his healing ability away makes Logan vulnerable, which is refreshing. He is still as indestructible as most action stars, but it's nice to see something at least be a challenge for him.

Disparities from the original comics aside, where the movie falls flat is its third act. We learn that Yashida faked his death and is being kept alive by a giant armored suit of adamantium so preposterous that it looks like Megatron had a baby with Shredder from the Michael Bay version of *Ninja Turtles*. Yashida's plan is to chop off Wolverine's claws and suck his healing powers out from his bones. It's an over-the-top culmination to what had (mostly) been a dramatic chase movie and is incongruous with the rest of the film. It's also a poor payoff to what the movie is *really* about: an immortal struggling to find fulfillment and purpose in a life that may never end.

The bible refers to a man who might have been able to relate to Logan and the weight that potentially everlasting life put on his shoulders, Methuselah. Genesis 5:27 says he lived to be 969, having fathered some children and ... that's it. Scripture never mentions him again. Scholars debate over whether the long lifespans of biblical figures were accurate. Some posit that their idea of a year was only a percentage of a full year, placing Methuselah at between 78 and 96. But if that were the case, it means other biblical fathers would have been children when they sired their own children.

Let us suppose Methuselah really was 969 years old. Imagine living nearly a millennium and having nothing said of your life except that you had a few children. His wisdom and stories should fill volumes, and yet he's only a footnote. Sadly, that's more than most get. What's better, I wonder; to live an unremarkable eternity or live a brief life of meaning?

Wolverine has some things in common with another person from the bible: Samson. He even looked like Samson in the film's beginning, with his long hair and beard, and was also shaved against his will. Both are invulnerable heroes who lose their powers, stand against countless foes, and are the best there is at what they do.

The bible has a lot to say about Samson's 20 years as a Judge, considering how little it says about Methuselah. No one knows how many years we'll get. Some will live to a ripe age, others will be cut down in their prime. But none of us are adamantine. We all die; the question is how do we live?

Though we look to eternity after death, our time on Earth is comparatively short. Some conserve their years but do nothing with them, others burn through them. You don't have to be immortal to live forever, though, if you carve a legacy. We might not have adamantium claws, but God can equip us to do uncanny things and leave a mark regardless. He will also help us to be the best there is at what we do, if what we do is honor Him.

JOURNAL QUESTIONS
- What gives your life fulfillment?
- What would you wish to be remembered for?

~ 12 ~
THE PUNISHER

"Come on God, answer me. For years I've asked why, why are the innocent dead and the guilty alive? Where is justice? Where is punishment? Or have you already answered? Have you already said to the world 'here is justice, here is punishment,' here, in me?"

Year: 1989
Distributor: New World Pictures
Producer: Robert Mark Kamen
Director: Mark Goldblatt
Writer: Boaz Yakin
Runtime: 89 minutes
Rating: Not Rated, includes graphic violence, language, and partial nudity.

Scripture Reading: Ezekiel 18:1-20

Dolph Lundgren is Frank Castle, a former cop who is driven to vigilantism by the murder of his family. Castle has declared a one-man war on crime but goes on a mission to rescue the children of the mob bosses he hunts after they are kidnapped by the Yakuza.

It may surprise you, but this is my favorite big screen version of Punisher (in spite of the fact that it wasn't shown on the big screen in America). The plot's thin, it lacks range, and the acting is questionable, but I love the Punisher as a gonzo, 80s shoot-em-up, because, to me, that's who Frank is. Though it screened overseas, New World Pictures could not afford a US theatrical release, so it went straight to video in 1991. Audience tastes were changing; violent antiheroes had become passé, so *Punisher* largely gathered dust on shelves.

Rather than a belabored origin like the 2004 movie, this film jumps right into the action. Frank has already been 'punishing' for five years. As if the Punisher wasn't enough, the local crime families are terrorized by a new threat, the Yakuza, led by the ruthless Lady Tanaka. She kidnaps the children of the local bosses under threat of selling them into slavery. In a curious twist, Frank sets out to save them, even though he has no problem killing their parents. To Frank, the children are innocent and deserve a chance, illustrating today's scripture reading, in which God says children are not accountable for the sins of their parents, nor are parents responsible for their children's.

The head of the cartel is Franco, whose son Tommy is in Tanaka's clutches. The relationship between he and and his son is nicely set up, and the film does a good job of making you think Franco might turn over a new leaf, but it's a double cross. The finale is a standoff between Castle, Franco, and the boy. Castle kills Franco, but Tommy pulls a gun on him. Castle kneels downs to let Tommy kill him, saying that it is better for him to get it over with than grow up and become like his father. Tommy relents, and Castle tells him that he is a good kid but warns if he doesn't grow into a good man, he'll be somewhere out there, watching.

In my book, *The Monster Gospels*, I elaborate on Exodus 20:1-7, which states that God punishes children (and even grandchildren) for the sins of their parents.[1] How do we reconcile that passage with today's reading? In *Monster Gospels*, I explain that our parents' sins create a pattern that we perpetuate with our choices. We *invite* punishment, not for our parents' sins but for sins we learned from them and then commit ourselves.

It could be argued that God broke His own rule by shouldering the punishment for the sins of the world in the person of Jesus, but Christ is not the Son of God only; He is also the Son of Man. He might not have committed sins but was still under the curse of sin. This is why in Mark 10:18 He rejected being called good. He was blameless, but human;

sinless, but became Sin for us (1 Corinthians 5:21), and His punishment is our acquittal.

Galatians 6:1-3 tells us "if someone is caught in a sin, you who live by the Spirit should restore that person gently. But watch yourselves, or you also may be tempted. Carry each other's burdens, and in this way you will fulfill the law of Christ. If anyone thinks they are something when they are not, they deceive themselves." Castle thinks he is entitled to be an executioner. That's *his* self-deception. His greatest act isn't killing mobsters, it's giving Tommy a chance. Proverbs 22:6 says "Start children off on the way they should go, and even when they are old they will not turn from it." In this act, Frank starts Tommy's new life off right.

Just as Castle gave Tommy a clean slate, God gives us a clean slate too. We can either return to the example of sin set forth by our mortal ancestry or we can let God use us as an answer to the injustices of the world. But unlike Castle, we shouldn't be out looking for someone to punish, but to reconcile, tempering Justice with Grace.

JOURNAL QUESTIONS

- Do you ever judge others by their family or friends?
- How can we be examples of Justice, tempered with Grace?

~ 13 ~
BATMAN: THE MOVIE

"Some days, you just can't get rid of a bomb."

Year: 1966
Distributor: 20th Century Fox
Producer: William Dozier
Director: Leslie H. Martinson
Writer: Lorenzo Semple Jr.
Runtime: 105 minutes
Rating: Approved

Scripture Reading: Ecclesiastes 12:1-8

Originally intended to debut *before* the premiere of the classic 60s *Batman* television series, *Batman: The Movie* was produced and released in between the first and second seasons of the show, instead. It features most of the series' cast, excepting Julie Newmar, whose role as Catwoman was taken over by Lee Meriwether. In the movie, Batman's four archenemies – Joker, Penguin, Riddler, and Catwoman – join forces to steal a dehydration ray in the hopes of holding the world's leaders hostage for billions in ransom.

The 60s interpretation of Batman is polarizing with

comic book fans. West, Ward, and Co. have been blanketed over by some like the white greasepaint on Caesar Romero's mustache. Which is to say, unsuccessfully. Those who grew up in a Post-Burton Batscape, or at least who read comics, recoil at the silliness of the cartoonish "pow" bubbles or the Boy-Wonder's incessant "Holy (blank)" puns. At best, they dismiss the series as a naïve misunderstanding of the source material made in a simpler era. Others revile the show as a cruel parody, mocking the very fan base it seeks to exploit. These detractors are quick to forget the frivolity of comics at the time. It's true that early *Batman* comics were darker, but by the time the 60s rolled around it was another story.

The movie has a dedication screen which informs us who it was made for: "to lovers of adventure, lovers of pure escapism, lovers of unadulterated entertainment, lovers of the ridiculous and the bizarre – to fun lovers everywhere." In short, this film and its caped crusaders aren't meant to be taken seriously; they're meant to be *fun*, and its turbines are most definitely "to speed" in that endeavor. Whether it's the ludicrous penguin submarine or Batman trying to get rid of a giant bomb or fend off a more convincing shark than any of the effects in *Sharknado*, this film embraces its absurdity as tenaciously as its critics forsake it. Even its DVD case is misleading, trading the bright colors of the film for a black background featuring nothing but cold, metallic letters and a simple red bat-symbol. It's as if the studio is ashamed of it and wants to trick buyers into thinking they are getting the 1989 film, instead.

The movie is about a dehydration ray. The fearsome foes use the ray to dehydrate the leaders of the United World Security Council, turning them into piles of dust that they plan to ransom for $1 billion each. The dynamic duo defeat the villains in a fight atop the Penguin's submarine, with all the sound effect graphics that made the show a classic. They reconstitute the leaders, but as soon as they are re-hydrated they go back to arguing as if nothing happened. The twist is that some of their dusts mingled, swapping their voices and points of view. Batman notes that this involuntary meeting of the minds might be the single greatest gift to the world.

We all are dust and will return to the dust one day. Though this film reminds of that, we're also reminded of it every year on Ash Wednesday, the beginning of Lent. One common Ash Wednesday scripture is Psalm 103:13-14, which reads, "As a father has compassion on his children, so the LORD has compassion on those who fear him; for he knows how we are formed, he remembers that we are dust."

Like film versions of Batman, life grows darker as the years wear on; today's scripture encourages us to remember God in the carefree days of our youth, because cultivating a connection to Him when times are good gives us perspective for when times are not. It also gives us a sense of proportion so that we don't get overwhelmed by circumstances that may not be as dire as they appear.

You might like more 'dark' in your Dark Knight, but there are plenty of somber iterations out there. Adam West represented the 'carefree days' of Batman, and those days are worth remembering. He isn't *gritty*, but he reminds us we're dust. As dust, we can afford to take ourselves, and the foibles of others, a little less seriously.

Sadly, West passed away, but his Batman lives on in a new animated film starring he, Ward, and Newmar, as well as new comics and merchandise based off of the series. The movie might have only grossed $1.7 million against a $1.5 million budget, but its effects are still felt, proving that this is one 'bomb' that really *is* hard to get rid of.

JOURNAL QUESTIONS
- What style of Batman do you prefer? Why?
- How can taking ourselves less seriously help our ministry?

~ 14 ~
SUPERGIRL

"Such a pretty world. I can't wait until
it's all mine."

Year: 1984
Distributor: New World Pictures
Producer: Robert Mark Kamen
Director: Jeannot Szwarc
Writer: Boaz Yakin
Runtime: 89 minutes
Rating: Not Rated

Scripture Reading: Isaiah 47:8-14

Widely considered to be one of the worst superhero movies, *Supergirl* tells the story of Superman's cousin, Kara. She lives in a Kryptonian city which survived destruction by slipping into a pocket dimension by way of a magical sphere called the omegahedron. An artist named Zaltar 'borrows' the orb and lets Kara play with it, but it has a mind of its own and escapes to Earth. There, it falls into the hands of a would-be sorceress with delusions of grandeur.

The movie has significant problems, not the least of

which is that the plot keeps changing. At first, the movie is about Kara on a life or death quest to find the omegahedron and save her home, but then she stumbles across (I assume) a Quidditch game between Slytherin and Gryffindor, as their uniforms are green and burgundy, respectively, and because a warlock works at the school as a teacher. Kara enrolls, for some reason, and the film becomes a fish-out-of-water school comedy. Selena, the sorceress, starts out wanting to rule the world but gets sidetracked in a love triangle with a gardener whom she tries to bewitch.

Some choices are head-scratchingly dumb, like Kara pretending to be Clark Kent's cousin to get into the school, even writing a letter of recommendation from him when the Dean isn't looking. How does she know who Clark Kent is, or, for that matter, English? Other parts are cringe-inducing, like having her roommate be Lois Lane's kid sister, Lucy.

For its many faults, the film has *some* good qualities. Helen Slater looks like Supergirl came to life right out of the comics, and she exudes enough kindness and confidence to be convincing. It also has a more exciting soundtrack than a lot of *good* superhero movies. Faye Dunaway is criminally wasted as Selena, as magic is one of the few weaknesses that a Kryptonian like Supergirl has and had never been explored on-screen. Blowing the opportunity to do so on silly parlor tricks is unfortunate, but supplies a few legitimately decent action scenes pitting Supergirl against the demon that Selena conjures to do her bidding.

Selena's undoing was her faulty assertion that the evil spirit she was summoning to fight Supergirl was subservient to her. She was toying with powers she didn't comprehend, and eventually the demon turns against her. Today's passage, similarly, makes plain the primary pitfall of practitioners of prestidigitation; you're not really the one who is in control.

You've heard, "it's better to rule in hell than serve in heaven," but the truth is, there's no ruling; just suffering. We catch a glimpse of what hell might be like when Selena sends Supergirl to the Phantom Zone. There, she finds Zaltar, who has been banished for losing the omegahedron. He explains that it isn't impossible to get out, but most won't try because the way is treacherous. By focusing on the light at the end of the tunnel rather than the challenges, Supergirl escapes.

Sorcery shifts the source of our trust to ourselves and our personal power instead of depending on God. Modern forms of sorcery don't usually involve conjuring spells or making potions like Selena, of course, but how many people do you know, maybe even *Christians*, who live by astrology and horoscopes? I don't think that God will banish you to the Phantom Zone for reading your horoscope and having a laugh, but He might grow concerned if you build your life around it. In fact, many self-declared witches believe in God, and some Christians incorporate spiritualist practices into their worship. That said, I'm reminded of Isaiah 8:19, where the prophet questions those who turn to those things, asking why one would seek wisdom from the dead rather than from a living God. Such logic is as convoluted as this movie.

The bible never says these practices don't work, only that we shouldn't use them. This is because, whatever form it takes, sorcery reveals a lack of faith; if you truly believe on Christ, you won't need answers elsewhere. For you, it might not be horoscopes or crystals, but there are plenty of other omegehedrons out there that give us a false sense of control. Chasing them veers us off course like the plot of this movie, but when we focus on God's wisdom rather our own power, we won't get stuck the Phantom Zone of spiritualism.

JOURNAL QUESTIONS
- Where do you find your greatest sense of security?
- What modern forms of "sorcery" might be a distraction for Christians? Have they been a distraction for you?

~ 15 ~
GREEN LANTERN

"Fear is the enemy of will. Will is what makes you take action; fear is what stops you and makes you weak, makes your constructs feeble."

Year: 2011
Distributor: Warner Bros. Pictures
Producers: Donald De Line, Greg Berlanti
Director: Martin Campbell
Writers: Greg Berlanti, Michael Green, Mark Guggenheim, and Michael Goldenberg
Runtime: 114 minutes
Rating: PG-13 for sequences of intense action, and some suggestive content

Scripture Reading: Matthew 7:24-27

Hal Jordan is a pilot whose life is forever changed when a dying alien offers him an emerald lantern and a ring that gives him the ability to construct whatever he imagines from pure energy, and the responsibility to use these gifts as a part of the Green Lantern Corps. The Lanterns are space police who defend the universe. The source of their power is pure Will, which they use against threats such as Parallax, an ancient enemy who has harnessed the power of Fear. Parallax is on a campaign to destroy Earth and then Oa, the Green Lantern home world, by feeding on the fear of others. The Guardians of Oa, immortal beings who created the rings and lead the Corps, are silent as Parallax gains momentum.

The primary ability of the rings allows its wearers to forge "constructs" of energy. In the film, Hal makes F-35's to fly him through space, catapults to send Parallax's attacks back at him, and even a giant-scale toy racetrack to move a helicopter to safety. The durability of the constructs depend on the user's willpower. What the ring can create is limited only by the imagination of the one who wears it, though the rings need to be energized by the lantern, like a battery.

Jesus talks about two 'constructs' in today's passage. One house is built on rock, the other sand. The house built on rock, which is to say that its foundation was on the Lord, withstood life's storms. Why? Because the confidence of the builder depended on a power more stable than himself. The other builder's house was only as strong as his ability. The problem is that our abilities have limits and are susceptible to doubt. As it happens, *doubt* is another way of saying *fear*, the principal weakness of a Green Lantern; fear is also the principal obstacle to faith.

Obstacles challenge us, but they don't have to defeat us. Fear tests faith, but it only has power if we give in to it. In the film, the Guardians create a yellow, fear ring thinking they can fight fear with fear, but Hal warns that if they cross that line and give in to fear, then they will never come back from that mindset. Too often, we're taught that fear is a sign of weakness, so we become as stoic as the Guardians, afraid of admitting that we are afraid. This, Hal declares, is why Parallax is winning; rather than drawing from their source, the Guardians are depending on their own strength, which has been undermined by fear.

In the same way that *doubt* is a synonym for *fear*, a synonym for *will* is *faith*. As Christians, we sadly can't make constructs out of energy, but we *can* perform miracles. Jesus said in John 14:12 that we could perform *even greater* ones than He, because He was going back to the Father. In fact, He says in Matthew 17:20 that with the smallest amount of faith we could move mountains. We often think faith is just belief, but it's more. Faith is *trust*. Maintaining mountain-moving amounts of faith requires connection to our creator.

Just as the ring needs to be energized by the lantern, we need the Holy Spirit to reinvigorate us. His power is our strength (Ephesians 6:10) much like the green energy of Will is the power source for the Lanterns. When life's Parallaxes disparage us, God's Word is *our* lantern, lighting our path (Psalm 119:105). We can be bold in spite of our fear, because perfect love drives off fear, and God *is* Love.

What is your 'source?' Do you find that you depend more on the Lord's strength or your own? Proverbs 3:5-6 says that we should lean on the Lord rather than on our own understanding, and that if we're willing to honor Him in all we do, then He will straighten our paths. The challenge is that some of us are *really* good at taking care of ourselves. Like Hal Jordan in his cockpit, we can feel like untouchable flying aces. It's hard to recognize a need for a higher source when we're accustomed to constructing our lives however we wish, but God can inspire us to build far greater things than we can imagine if we make His wisdom our foundation, His power our source, and His Word our blueprint.

JOURNAL QUESTIONS
- What are some threats to your willpower?
- What are some ways to safeguard against unhealthy doubts?

~ 16 ~
IRON MAN

"I had my eyes opened. I came to realize that I had more to offer this world than just making things that blow up."

Year: 2008
Distributor: Paramount Pictures
Producers: Avi Arad, Kevin Feige
Director: Jon Favreau
Writers: Matt Fergus, Hawk Ostby, Art Marcum, Matt Halloway
Runtime: 126 minutes
Rating: PG-13 for some intense sequences of sci-fi action and violence, and brief suggestive content

Scripture Reading: Galatians 6:7-9

The flagship of the Marvel Cinematic Universe, this film had a lot riding on it. *Iron Man* would need to both set up Tony Stark and his franchise *and* serve as the launch pad for the rest of Marvel's roster of heroes. In a way, *Iron Man* was as important for the future of comic book movies as the original *Superman* was to establishing their legitimacy. *Iron Man* accomplishes its Herculean goal, setting the standard for superhero movies for the following decade.

Tony Stark is a brilliant weapons developer who lives fast and has little regard for others. After demonstrating his newest weapon, the Jericho Missile, Tony is ambushed by a terrorist group called the Ten Rings, an allusion to a classic comic book villain named the Mandarin who is famous for his ten magical rings. The attack leaves shrapnel in his heart, which is kept at bay by an electromagnet attached to a car battery, installed by a fellow scientist who's also been taken prisoner. Tony learns that the terrorists have weapons from his company and want him to build them more. He designs a suit of armor and an updated power source for his heart, instead, overpowering his captors and escaping.

Once home, Stark decides to shut down all weapons production, which is a shock to his partner, Obidiah Stane. Stane puts Tony on house arrest, so to speak, until the media debacle blows over and stocks stabilize. This gives Tony time for his true purpose: upgrading his suit and rounding up his weapons from the terrorists. It turns out that Stane was the one selling them; he is also building his own suit to rival Tony's as a prototype for the military. They duke it out and Iron Man triumphs. Then, Tony holds a press conference to offer a cover and tell everyone that Iron Man is his personal bodyguard but, in stark contrast to the conventions of the genre, confesses that he is Iron Man, instead.

Iron Man is the story of a man who reaped what he sowed but decides to make it right. The film itself sowed the template for what every Marvel movie would be, and it has reaped a fortune. As of this writing, the Marvel Cinematic Universe has grossed $4.5 *billion.*[1] It's almost as if this film is an allegory for superhero movies, which had become self-important and pedantic. At a time when the only successful superhero films were 'dark and gritty,' *Iron Man* proved that superhero flicks could be profitable and *fun.*

Another allegory that begins in a cave was written by Plato. Someone who spent his life chained to a cave wall looking at shadow puppets gets out and sees the real world, forever changing his perceptions. Tony's experience in a cave changes him too, and once his eyes were opened he couldn't go back to who he was before. We all start in a cave, settling for lesser lights that pass for reality until we witness God's. Some go back to the comfort of that cave; others go back to free more captives.

Once free from the cave, Tony begins to think over his life and legacy. Proverbs 28:13 reads, "Whoever conceals their sins does not prosper, but the one who confesses and renounces them finds mercy." I can't think of any hero who typifies this better than Tony Stark, or, for that matter, actor Robert Downey Jr., who escaped his own cave of recklessness and addiction but is now blazing a very different legacy with his career thanks to his public repentance.

Everything we do plants a seed. We sow destruction if we reap it (Job 4:8), but we harvest eternity if we sow our spirits (Galatians 6:8). We reap bountifully if we sow liberally (2 Corinthians 9:6), but we reap nothing if we sow nothing. Luckily, this movie shows us that even if we plant a bitter harvest we can uproot and try again. God, and *Iron Man*, are all about second chances.

Just like the world is bigger than Plato's cave, Tony's world gets bigger when he is visited by Nick Fury, director of S.H.I.E.L.D.. Fury comes to tell Tony that he is part of a larger universe and invites him to join the Avengers. We are also part of a larger Body, and we achieve more when we join forces with other field workers. But first, we have to get out of our cave and realize the world is bigger than us.

JOURNAL QUESTIONS
- Have you had a life-changing "spiritual cave" experience?
- What legacy do your choices foreshadow? Is that the legacy you wish to leave? If not, how can you change course?

~ 17 ~
THE INCREDIBLE HULK

"I don't want to control it. I want to get rid of it."

Year: 2008
Distributor: Universal Pictures
Producers: Avi Arad, Gale Anne Hurd, Kevin Feige
Director: Louis Leterrier
Writer: Zak Penn
Runtime: 112 minutes
Rating: PG-13 for sequences of intense action violence, some frightening sci-fi images, and brief suggestive content

Scripture Reading: James 1:19-20

The second attempt at a big-screen version of the jade giant, and the second entry in the MCU, *The Incredible Hulk* ignores the 2003 Ang Lee film and draws inspiration from the 1970s TV series starring Bill Bixby. Bruce Banner is on the run and in search of a cure while reconnecting with his lost love, Betty Ross, and avoiding her father, General "Thunderbolt" Ross. Banner is also being tracked by Emil Blonsky, a soldier whose descent into madness turns him into the monstrous Abomination.

The film effectively establishes its own backstory in its opening credits in the form of violent flashbacks, which reveal that Bruce subjected himself to tests using a gamma radiation device invented by Betty and he. He turns into the Hulk, and General Ross wants to capture him. Banner goes on the run, leaving Betty (and his old life) behind. We begin the film in Brazil, where Bruce is laying low working for a soda factory and communicating through messages on the web with a stranger who claims to be able to help. A freak accident at the factory leads to a cameo by Hulk creator Stan Lee, who is infected by a bottle of soda tainted with Bruce's blood. This leads Thunderbolt Ross to Brazil to catch him.

Bruce returns to the US, where he meets with Betty and the scientist he's been communicating with online. The scientist, Dr. Samuel Sterns, used a sample of Bruce's blood to produce gallons of it, which he intends to use for various experiments. Dogging Bruce's steps is Emil Blonsky, an egomaniacal soldier who's juiced himself up on the same serum that powered Captain America. He convinces Sterns to give him an injection of Bruce's blood, which mutates him into the Abomination and sets the stage for a climactic fight in Harlem between him and the Hulk.

From the gamma gizmo that turns Banner into the

Hulk, the close-ups of his glowing eyes before he changes, the melodic "Lonely Man" piano jingle (and even a clip of Bixby from his other show, *The Magician)*, this film draws a lot from the classic TV show. Even original Hulk actor Lou Ferrigno makes a cameo. The movie captures the feeling of watching the show, focusing on the struggle of a man who is on the run both figuratively and literally. Bruce doesn't care about learning how to control the Hulk, he just wants to get rid of him.

The bible has several passages on the subject of anger and losing one's temper. Proverbs 29:11 says that wise people know when to hold back, and that only fools let themselves "give full vent to their anger." Ephesians 4:26 clarifies that it's okay to be *angry*, just don't sin as a result of it. That's because, as today's verse says, human anger doesn't produce Godly righteousness. Bruce's issue isn't anger, though; it's a lack of self-control. If Bruce were in control of himself, then the Hulk wouldn't matter, but he runs because he's afraid of what he's capable of.

A lot of us run from temptation. Even Paul says to flee from it in 1 Corinthians 6:18, but he concedes in 10:13 that God doesn't allow us to be tempted beyond our ability to endure. We can never know what we can endure, however, if we don't confront our sources of temptation. We are slaves to sin even if we don't give in for no other reason than we're more afraid of it than we are confident in God's power to keep us from Hulking out.

One area in which some believers struggle not to give "full vent to their anger" is on the internet. They joke about Christians on highways, but it's worse on the Information Superhighway, where some of us have no qualms lashing out at others under the pretense of 'righteous indignation.' Jesus said hating our neighbors is the same as murder; that applies to our comments towards them online. God sees what we do in secret (Matthew 6:6), which includes the internet, despite how anonymous we think we are. We can also put too much of ourselves out there on the web, like Bruce, who unwisely gives his irradiated blood to a stranger.

Whether online or in person, we must be diligent. A person without self-control is like a city with a broken wall: exposed (Proverbs 25:28). We *can* use our anger productively, we just have to learn how to aim it.

JOURNAL QUESTIONS
- Are your online interactions consistent with your values?
- Where do you struggle to maintain your temper most?

~ 18 ~
IRON MAN 2

"Contrary to popular belief, I know exactly what I'm doing."

Year: 2010
Distributor: Paramount Pictures
Producer: Kevin Feige
Director: Jon Favreau
Writers: Justin Theroux
Runtime: 124 minutes
Rating: PG-13 for sequences of intense sci-fi action and violence, and some language

Scripture Reading: 2 Corinthians 12:7-10

The *Rocky III* of superhero movies in that it's about a superstar's fall from grace, but also the *Rocky IV* of superhero movies in that its villain is a big, monosyllabic Russian stereotype, *Iron Man 2* picks up where the first film left off; at a press conference in which Tony Stark admits that he is Iron Man. This time, we see it from a different perspective, the television of a dying Russian scientist who designed the arc reactor with Stark's father, Howard. Cast out of the US and never given credit, he then dies in poverty having seen his greatest invention actualized. This outrages his son, Ivan Vanko, who vows revenge.

Vanko might not need to try too hard, as things have taken a turn for Tony since last we saw him. On the surface, he appears to be drunk on his own success, but, as the layers of bravado peel back, we learn he's dying; the arc reactor in his chest is poisoning him. Causing additional worry is the government cracking down and trying to confiscate his suit, viewing it as a weapon that belongs in military hands. He is also harried by Justin Hammer, a rival tech developer played brilliantly by Sam Rockwell, who is looking for any means to one-up Stark. His prayer is answered when Vanko appears on the scene, wielding dual whips powered by an arc reactor. Hammer decides to fund Vanko as a "silent backer" on the condition that Vanko helps him make Iron Man obsolete.

Vanko's goal isn't to kill Tony but destroy his legacy and break his ego. His view is that "if you could make God bleed, people would cease to believe in Him." Expose Stark's vulnerabilities, and the "sharks" will come sniffing.

The problem with this reasoning is that someone *did* make God bleed. Someone beat Him and put a crown of thorns on His head. Someone nailed spikes into His hands and feet, hung Him on a cross, and then stuck a spear into

His side just to make sure He was dead. After his dramatic entrance into the Stark Expo, Tony declares that he is the greatest personification of a phoenix metaphor, but Jesus is the one who literally died and came back; Jesus is the God who bled, and it only made people believe in Him more.

After considering with his assistant, Natalie, how to spend what might be his final birthday, Tony has a drunken boxing match with his friend Rhodey, then flies off. Tony's discovered the next morning by Nick Fury and Natalie, who is actually a S.H.I.E.L.D. agent keeping tabs on him named Natasha Romanoff. Nick tells Tony that the solution to his problem is in his late father's work. After some digging, he discovers that Howard left him a roadmap to a new element, a project he couldn't complete in his lifetime. Tony creates the element, which cures his poisoning. In a rare moment of humility, Tony concedes that, even after all these years, his dad was still taking him to school.

Tony is a narcissist; it's difficult for him to ask for or receive help. Had Fury not tipped Tony off, Hammer and Vanko would likely have won because of Tony's arrogance. Self-sufficiency is a virtue, but it tricks us into thinking we don't need God; it also tricks us into thinking we don't need others. We have discussed the importance of teamwork, but the most challenging part of teamwork is being willing to receive help. There's no award for being a better martyr than Jesus; our armors accomplish nothing but proving we aren't *actually* self-sufficient.

I never battled arc reactor poisoning, but I did have a medical issue recently that required blood work, and I wasn't terribly motivated to do it. The pleas of my friends did not help, but one of them, my editor, had a sneaky strategy; he refused to give me my revised manuscript until I got it done. He knew the chink in *my* armor – my work – and did what was necessary to help me. *That's* friendship.

We don't know if it was a medical issue, like what I had to deal with, but Paul describes a thorn in his flesh that keeps him humble in today's scripture. Tony has one as well: shrapnel inching towards his heart that the arc reactor keeps at bay. His best effort was killing him; it took accepting help from others to find healing. Likewise, our support network is useless if we don't let anyone through our armor.

JOURNAL QUESTIONS

- How good are you with receiving help? Why is it important that we learn to do so?
- How would you celebrate your birthday if it was your last?

~ 19 ~
THOR

"Whosoever holds this hammer, if he be worthy, shall possess the power of Thor."

Year: 2011
Distributor: Paramount Pictures
Producer: Kevin Feige
Director: Kenneth Branagh
Writers: Ashley Miller, Zack, Stentz, Don Payne
Runtime: 115 minutes
Rating: PG-13 for sequences of intense sci-fi action and violence

Scripture Reading: James 4:1-3

Of all the films in Phase One of the MCU, before we even knew there *were* 'Phases,' today's film seemed like it would be the hardest sell. Other superhero movies were just people in suits or science accidents turned super-hero. Even aliens didn't seem too far-fetched, but ancient Norse gods? How would they make *that* work? Like others, I feared that *Thor* was where the burgeoning Marvel Cinematic Universe would screech to a halt.

Director Kenneth Branagh makes Thor's debut work

in spite of its fantasy elements by grounding the story in the dynamic between he and his mischievous brother, Loki. As the director of *Much Ado About Nothing, Hamlet, Henry V,* and *A Midwinter's Tale,* it's clear why they chose Branagh; he has a knack for making the ponderous accessible. Sillier aspects of Norse mythology, such as the Rainbow Bridge, are handled with care. Until Thor smashes it, anyway.

Thor is a brazen fighter preparing to become king of Asgard. Odin, the Allfather, is about to crown him when Frost Giants break into the castle vault in search of a relic Odin took after defeating them. Manipulated by Loki, Thor and his fellow warriors go to Jotunheim, the Frost Giants' home world, to teach them a lesson. Thor is the one to learn a lesson, however, after Odin casts him to Earth. Odin also sends Mjolnir, Thor's hammer, declaring that only someone worthy of its power will be able to wield it.

The subject of worthiness is as central to the bible as it is to *Thor.* We see worthiness first addressed in the story of Cain and Abel, two brothers as diametrically opposed as Loki and Thor. They offer sacrifices to God, but God only finds Abel's acceptable. He tells Cain that his offerings will be favored if he does what's right, but he kills Abel instead.

It is James, however, who scribed the central scripture

on worthiness, as well as a harsh opinion regarding why our desires go unmet; we ask for the purpose of self-indulgence. He goes so far as to state that we would be willing to *kill* for the things we desire. It seems extreme, but how often have *you* said "I'd kill for a (blank)." Sure, it's a joke, but a joke that articulates how badly we want something. James asserts that we don't have what we want because we don't ask God, and when we do ask He doesn't doesn't give it to us because of our motives.

It might not be a magical hammer, but many of us have a 'Mjolnir.' For Loki, though he does try unsuccessfully to claim the hammer, his 'Mjolnir' is the throne of Asgard. For you, it might be a job promotion that you keep getting passed over for, or perhaps it's the affection of someone you adore. Whatever it is, you *feel* worthy and don't understand why you don't have what you long for.

This sort of coveting is insidiously easy for believers who place too much importance on moral correctness. They think they deserve more because they honor God with their morals and forget that ours isn't a faith of deservedness but grace. God isn't impressed with our works; the only sacrifice He accepts is a contrite spirit (Psalm 51:17). Yet, we bargain. He doesn't seem to hear us, though, but how could He when we have placed something else on His throne?

One of my 'Mjolnirs' was the position of pastor at a small church where I served as youth pastor for seven years. I had been going through the process and was about to have my chance, but things didn't work out. I was devastated. The church had been through a rough transition which exposed a level of toxicity I was unaware of and, frankly, unprepared for. The divisiveness was still at work a year later when I left. In spite of some really wonderful people, I would have been miserable as the pastor of that church, I just didn't know it. God knew, and what I thought was punishment was actually protection. This event prompted me to leave career ministry and pursue writing, and I have never been happier.

Sometimes, the reason God does not give us what we ask for isn't because we aren't worthy of it; it isn't worthy of us. God always has a better Mjolnir in mind than we do. If we want to pick up that hammer, we first must lay down our crown.

JOURNAL QUESTIONS
- Describe a lesson you learned from not getting what you wanted. Did you ever get it? How do you feel, either way?
- What are some 'Mjonirs' in your life?

~ 20 ~
CAPTAIN AMERICA:
THE FIRST AVENGER

"Whatever happens tomorrow, you must promise me one thing: that you will stay who you are. Not a perfect soldier, but a good man."

Year: 2011
Distributor: Paramount Pictures
Producer: Avi Arad, Kevin Feige
Director: Joe Johnston
Writers: Christopher Markus and Stephen McFeely
Runtime: 124 minutes
Rating: PG-13 for intense sequences of sci-fi violence and action.

Scripture Reading: 2 Corinthians 9:24-27

Continuing the mystery of the Tesseract, a glowing blue cube first teased during the post-credits scene in *Thor*, *Captain America* introduces us to Steve Rogers, a tiny but good-hearted kid from Brooklyn turned Super Soldier. With his indestructible vibranium shield, he battles Red Skull, a Nazi who uses the Tesseract to power doomsday weapons.

The film opens in present day with the discovery of

Captain America buried under ice. We then go back to the past, where the wimpy Rogers flunks every attempt to enlist because of his myriad health issues and diminutive frame. His friend Bucky wishes he could be content staying back and serving in safer ways, but Rogers believes that he has no right to when others are laying down their lives.

This exchange is overheard by Dr. Abraham Erskine, who defected from Germany and now aids the US in a secret science division. He enrolls Rogers into his program, where Steve proves his mettle as a candidate for becoming a 'Super Soldier,' an experimental process that uses a serum to make him the pinnacle of health and fitness.

The night before the procedure, Rogers asks Erskine why he was selected for the process. Erskine explains that the serum amplifies all aspects of a person, inward and outward. The first to use it was Red Skull, whose disfigurement was a side effect. He was already a power-hungry lunatic, but the serum made him a would-be conqueror. Erskine chose Steve because "a strong man, who has known power all his life, may lose respect for that power, but a weak man knows the value of strength, and knows compassion."

One thing the movie doesn't do a very good job of explaining is the range of Steve's powers. Based on the film, you might think that Captain America is super-human, but that isn't so. According to the comics, Steve is merely at the apex of human potential. Theoretically, anyone able-bodied enough could become Captain America if he or she trained diligently. It calls to mind our passage today, in which Paul compares the discipline of following Jesus to an athlete who trains for a big race.

Grace is not a magic elixir that brings us to our full potential like the formula that powers Captain America; we have to be steady in our commitment to self-improvement. Grace simply gives us the opportunity to do so. Salvation is like Dr. Erskine's serum; it amplifies what is already there. A person who is lazy uses eternal security as an excuse to coast; a proud person uses it as a pennant to feel superior.

Captain America and Red Skull are at the same basic level of strength and ability. To continue the race analogy, if they were to compete, they would be evenly matched. What separates the two is what they fight for. The most sterling trophy will deteriorate, but what we as Christians strive for is eternal. The Red Skull wants world domination, but, if he succeeded, his reign would be a perishable bauble that would die with him. Captain America, conversely, battles for an ideal. Ideals are *lasting*.

Red Skull's hubris is his undoing; the Tesseract sends him to space, and Steve crashes a plane full of weapons into the ocean, sacrificing his life. This brings us back to present day, where Steve is revived and recruited into the Avengers, setting up tomorrow's entry.

Red Skull asks Steve why Erskine picked him, as he sees himself as superior. In Philippians 2:3, Paul says to "do nothing out of selfish ambition or vain conceit. Rather, in humility value others above yourselves." In 1 Corinthians 4:7, he asks a similar question as Red Skull, albeit to make a different point; "who makes you different from anyone else? What do you have that you did not receive? And if you did receive it, why do you boast as though you did not?"

Just as Steve's powers were a gift, everything we have comes from God. What matters is the substance of who we are underneath those gifts and the discipline we maintain to reach for excellence. Only once we understand this can we take up our own indestructible shield, the Shield of Faith, and enter the fray.

JOURNAL QUESTIONS
- How is personal discipline important for spiritual growth?
- What areas do you struggle with being conceited?

~ 21 ~
THE AVENGERS

"There's only one God, ma'am, and I'm pretty
sure he doesn't dress like that."

Year: 2012
Distributor: Paramount Pictures
Producer: Kevin Feige
Director: Joss Whedon
Writer: Joss Whedon
Runtime: 143 minutes
Rating: PG-13 for intense sequences of sci-fi violence and
action throughout, and a mild drug reference

Scripture Reading: 1 Peter 2:13-17

One of the highest-grossing movies of all time, this
film changed the game. The culmination of the five movies
which preceded it, *The Avengers* brings Iron Man, Captain
America, Thor, and the Hulk together to battle the deranged
Loki, who's stolen the Tesseract and uses it to open a portal
to a place where creatures called the Chitauri wait to destroy
Earth. Loki thinks he is a god, but the Hulk shows him just
how puny he really is by tossing him around like a rag doll
after the Avengers dispatch his army.

I remember seeing it for the first time with my dad and my friend Dave. I don't think I've ever been in such a spirited audience. I mainly remember how entranced my dad was; as the man who introduced me to these stories as a kid, he'd wanted to see a movie like this since he himself was a child. He nodded throughout the film at small touches, like Hulk not being able to pick up Mjolnir, and he swooned at the reveal of Thanos like Caulson over Captain America, a tease of something even grander than these six movies. The theater roared when Thanos turned and smirked. Dave, who isn't a comic guy, clapped along, baffled, then leaned in and whispered, "Why are we clapping?"

Loki is decidedly different this time around. He has a philosophy regarding mankind, that deep down we are made to be ruled and that freedom is a lie – a distraction keeping us in a mad scramble for purpose and identity. The thing is, Loki isn't entirely wrong; not from a biblical point of view, anyway. The first of the Ten Commandments is a mandate to put nothing ahead of our devotion to God, and Psalms is filled with orders to sing God's praises. In both Isaiah and Revelation, God's throne is surrounded by heavenly beings who do nothing but say "holy, holy, holy" in His presence. In Isaiah 45, God vows that every knee will eventually kneel before Him, and Philippians 2:10-11 echoes it, saying every knee should bow to Jesus and acknowledge that He's Lord.

It is clear, biblically, that God demands our worship, but is Loki correct that we were made to be *ruled?* Are these things the same? Psalm 29:2 says that worship is honoring God by giving Him due credit, and Hebrews 13:15 is similar in sentiment (a word you hear *a lot* in this movie), telling us to give "a sacrifice of praise." Jesus references Deuteronomy 6:13 to rebuke Satan in Luke 4:8, "Fear the LORD your God, serve him only and take your oaths in his name." Romans 12:1 also addresses service, saying that true, spiritual worship is offering our bodies as living sacrifices. There does seem to be an assumption of serving that comes with worship, so is freedom a lie? No. The lie is believing we were ever free.

We are born in bondage to sin (Psalm 51:5), but Jesus says in John 8:32 that Truth sets us free. What is His motive for freeing us, though? Galatians 5:1 says "it is for freedom that Christ has set us free." Jesus wants to be our Lord, not our ruler. Isaiah 9:6-7 says He will govern us one day, and that His government will have no end, but *governing* is not the same as *ruling.* States have governors, and their job is to protect us and our liberties. Jesus liberates us from sin, and then protects that liberty as our spiritual governor, but our citizenship in the kingdom is voluntary. Nick Fury couldn't *make* Tony, Steve, or Bruce join the Avengers, but once they enlisted they fell under his authority. Likewise, God will not force us accept His invitation, but accepting carries with it certain expectations.

Whether or not Loki opened the portal, the Chitauri were there waiting to get in. Similarly, unseen spiritual forces around us wait for a foothold. We can use our freedom to ignore that, or as an opportunity to serve. In the film, Nick explains the Avengers to Captain America, that "the idea was to bring together a group of of remarkable people to see if they could become something more." God doesn't want to rule us; like Captain America giving the Hulk permission to smash, He wants to set us loose. That's the kind of worship God is looking for; unleashing our potential in tandem with others for His purposes. And we don't have to fear the evil that waits like the Chitauri on the other side of the veil; our enemy has an army - we have a God, and He isn't puny.

JOURNAL QUESTIONS
- Do you feel that you are operating at your full potential? If not, what holds you back?
- How do you understand spiritual freedom?"

~ 22 ~
X-MEN: FIRST CLASS

"Mutant and Proud."

Year: 2011
Distributor: 20th Century Fox
Producers: Lauren Shuler Donner, Bryan Singer, Simon Kinberg, Gregory Goodman
Director: Matthew Vaugn
Writers: Ashley Edward Miller, Zack Stentz, Jane Goldman, Matthew Vaugn
Runtime: 132 minutes
Rating: PG-13 for intense sequences of action and violence, some sexual content including brief partial nudity and language

Scripture Reading: Matthew 9:38-41

After *X-Men: The Last Stand* seemed to have killed the franchise (along with half the original cast) and after the first *Wolverine* solo film failed to launch an *X-Men Origins* brand, *X-Men: First Class* offers a hip, 60s-era reboot which shows the blossoming friendship of Xavier and Magneto, as well as their parting of ways, set against the backdrop of the Cuban Missile Crisis. We also see the beginnings of the X-

Men as they fight Sebastian Shaw, who wants to start WWIII so he can eliminate humans and rule a world of mutants.

Erik "Magneto" Lensherr is on a mission in the film, cutting through former Nazis to get to Sebastian Shaw, the Nazi scientist who experimented on him and murdered his mother. Contrasting Erik and Shaw's position that mutants should rise above humans is Charles Xavier, who dreams of a peaceful coexistence. Torn between the two views is Raven, a mutant covered in blue scales who has the ability to look like other people. She hides behind the form of a beautiful, everyday teen to compensate for how ugly she feels inside.

Raven's struggle is being "Mutant and Proud," which is hard when everyone, even Charles, prefers that she use her power to appear "normal." Only Erik looks at her true form and sees perfection. She's in love with Xavier, but, because he took her in as a child, he claims to only be capable of seeing her as a sister. This hurts her, but she's then drawn by Erik's magnetism, joining him and becoming Mystique. After she chooses Erik, Mystique confronts Xavier, saying she thought it would be them against the world but sees that no matter how bad the world gets, he doesn't *want* to be against it.

Shaw has no problem being against the world. Like his pupil, Erik, he believes that a revolution is inevitable and that mutants will be enslaved unless they rise up to rule. He tries to woo the nascent X-Men to his side and warns if they are not with him, then they are against him.

Jesus makes two seemingly conflicting statements on this topic. In Matthew 12:30 He says, "Whoever is not with me is against me," but in our main passage He says the exact opposite, "whoever is not against us is for us." While some see this as a contradiction, the difference is in the context. In Matthew 12, Jesus is discussing the Church, that a house divided cannot stand, and that believers must be united. The other verse is about people outside of our faith circles. The disciples wanted to stop strangers from performing miracles in Jesus' name because they weren't part of their group, but Jesus corrected them. One is about unity in the Church, the other is about our relationship to those outside of it.

Just as it's hard for Raven to be "Mutant and Proud" in her culture, it can be hard to feel Christian and Proud in our own, which doesn't always seem to be "for us." Another mutant in the film is Hank McCoy. His mutation is minor, but he is completely ashamed of it. Both Raven and Charles encourage him to be himself, but he makes a serum from Raven's blood instead, hoping to suppress his mutation. It only mutates him further. Some believers are like Hank; they are ashamed of their faith and desperate to conceal it. James 4:4 calls this "friendship with the world," and it's what Jesus meant when He said that whoever is not with Him is against Him. Much like Hank's misguided efforts turned him into a beast, trying to fit in with the world turns us into something the Lord didn't intend and only makes us stick out more.

The movie's climax is a standoff between Cuban and US fleets. Neither want a war, but Shaw tries to instigate one anyway. Similarly, the "Shaws" of the church stir up trouble by forgetting that not being "friends with the world" doesn't justify being unfriendly towards the people who live in it. If they're not against us, Jesus says they're for us. Sometimes we invent enemies by confusing disagreement with hate. People can disagree with us and still support us, and we can do that for them too. Don't hide your faith; like Xavier encouraged Hank, you can show off. Just don't treat what sets us apart as an excuse to lord over others, like Shaw. Be Christian and Proud, not Christian and Prideful.

JOURNAL QUESTIONS
- Do you struggle more with friendship with the world or with spiritual pridefulness?
- How can we take pride in our faith without being prideful?

~ 23 ~
THE AMAZING SPIDER-MAN

"I had a professor once who liked to tell his students that there were only 10 different plots in all of fiction. Well, I'm here to tell you he was wrong. There is only one; 'Who am I?'"

Year: 2012
Distributor: Columbia Pictures
Producers: Avi Arad, Matt Tolmach, Laura Ziski
Director: Marc Webb
Writers: James Vanderbilt, Alvin Sargent, Steve Cloves
Runtime: 136 minutes
Rating: PG-13 for sequences of action and violence

Scripture Reading: Mark 3:1-6

Andrew Garfield shines as a funnier Spider-Man in a retelling of the hero's origin which focuses on the mystery of how Peter Parker became an orphan. He falls in love with Gwen Stacy, the daughter of the police captain hunting him, and inadvertently creates his own nemesis by helping a one-armed scientist who is studying cross-species genetics develop a formula that makes his arm grow back but then transforms him into a reptilian monster.

In an effort to distance itself from its predecessor, no one says "with great power comes great responsibility" in the film. Instead, Uncle Ben offers a clunky paraphrase, that "if you could do good things for other people, you had a moral obligation to do those things." It's a more specific message than the original and reminds me of a friend with whom I was discussing morality. He explained that his morality was not built around the philosophy of "do no harm," but was "make things better." To him, if we have the power to make things better, then we ought to. This sentiment is shared by the film's antagonist, Dr. Curt Connors.

Dr. Connors is a layered character in the comic, with a deep connection to Peter, and has a wife and son. All the movie tells us about Connors is that he wants to help others overcome their disabilities, obviously motivated by his own. Having given Curt the formula that transforms him into the Lizard, Peter feels honor-bound to stop him, not because he sees him as a monster but because he feels responsible.

Jesus has a similar opportunity to do good for a man with an arm disability in our scripture today. Unlike Curt, whose arm is completely missing, the man in our story's arm is withered. Before healing the man, Jesus asks a question of the Pharisees, who were looking for an excuse to arrest Him.

It was the Sabbath, a day of the week in which it was against the Law of Moses to do any work. Jesus essentially asks if it's more lawful to save someone on the Sabbath or to let them die. The Pharisees, unsurprisingly, stands silent, so Jesus asks the crippled man to extend his withered arm and suddenly it is healed. Instead of being awed by the miracle, the Pharisees plot how to destroy Christ.

In the film, Peter has a debate with Gwen's father, a police captain who wants to arrest Spider-Man because he is a vigilante. He is disinterested in Peter's position, who says that Spider-Man just wants to use his abilities to help. Like the Pharisees, Captain Stacy is more focused on the letter of the law than the heart. James 14:7 says that if we neglect to do the good we know we ought to do, then it's a sin for us, just as it would have been sin for Jesus to not heal the man when He had the opportunity to do so.

This is what makes Connors complicated. Once he becomes the Lizard, he plots to transform everyone else into reptiles, too. From his demented perspective, his plan not only seems sensible; it's the moral thing to do. Humans will be stronger, faster, able to heal, and find solidarity from the pack mentality that they otherwise lack. He confronts Peter during their school battle and tells him that he doesn't *have* to stop him, as if he honestly thinks Peter misunderstands his intentions. From Curt's point of view, *he* is the hero of the story, not Spider-Man.

As it happens, we have a little 'lizard' in us; our brain stem. Referred to as our "lizard brain," it's the primitive part of us responsible for impulses like hunger, fight or flight, and breeding; our baser instincts, which are *literally* at the back of our mind at all times.

Proverbs 16:2 says all our ways seem right to us but God weighs our heart. Luckily for us, God is gracious when our inner Lizard takes over and confuses our intentions. In Matthew 5:50, Jesus says to cut off our hand if it makes us sin. Curing Curt of his "lizard brain" required him to lose the arm he desperately worked for. Similarly, God will renew our minds if we are willing to sacrifice the unhealthy ways of thinking we grasp at. Then, He will give us discretion for how to use the great powers He's given us, because with great power ... well, you know.

JOURNAL QUESTIONS
- Have you ever had good intentions that did harm, instead?
- Have you had an opportunity to help someone but didn't? In hindsight, are you glad you didn't or do you regret it?

~ 24 ~
BATMAN BEGINS

"It's not who I am underneath, but what I do that defines me."

Year: 2005
Distributor: Warner Bros.
Producers: Charles Rovan, Emma Thomas, Larry Franco
Director: Christopher Nolan
Writers: Christopher and David S. Goyer
Runtime: 140 minutes
Rating: PG-13 for intense action violence, disturbing images and some thematic elements

Scripture Reading: James 2:14-26

After 1997's universally panned *Batman & Robin*, things looked bleak for the Dark Knight. Nearly a decade later, *Batman Begins* debuted to much praise; the film not only reinvigorated faith in the Bat-brand with its thoughtful and intense portrayal of the source material but also proved once again that superhero movies could be dramatic. We see the process of Batman training and creating his dual identity for the first time in live action form as he battles Scarecrow and Ra's Al Ghul, also making their big screen debut.

As heavy on drama as it is with flashbacks, *Batman Begins* is the serious approach to the character that fans had always wanted. I remember the chills I felt at the scene when Batman scoops dirty cop Flass up to interrogate him, or as the Batmobile (called the Tumbler) vaults on rooftops. It was refreshing to meet a more dynamic Alfred, one with whom Bruce has a strained relationship, and it was thrilling to see nods to other adaptations. Scarecrow poisoning Gotham's water and seeing Batman as a demon after being exposed to his own fear toxin, for example, was pulled straight out of *Batman: The Animated Series.* I was also surprised that the film had a message.

After the success of *Spider-Man*, it was common for superhero films to shoehorn a 'moral' that wasn't otherwise there. *Daredevil, Ghost Rider,* and *Man of Steel* are all prime examples, and today's film is no exception. Were filmmakers so moved by *Spider-Man's* line that "with great power comes great responsibility" that they demanded every other hero get a 'Spider-Man,' too? Batman wasn't immune, either. In fact, there are so many 'Spider-Mans' in today's film that it's hard to choose. Apparently, the only thing director Christopher Nolan likes more than landscape shots and choppy edits is reincorporating moralizing dialogue. But for our purposes, I think Batman's assertion that it isn't who he is underneath but what he does that defines him is the main 'Spider-Man' of the movie.

Batman didn't come up with it on his own, though. His childhood friend (and current Assistant D.A.) Rachael says it when she sees him frolic with supermodels at a hotel restaurant. Bruce's public life as a playboy is an act. He tries to convince Rachael that there's more to him inside, but she says that what we do is more important than inner qualities.

James concurs in today's verse, his famous treatise on the distinction between faith and works. He is speaking to two groups: those who don't do any good works but absolve themselves by saying they don't need to because they have faith, and legalistic believers who cling to the Law and boast of their works as if it were a means of salvation.

To James, faith without works is dead, which is to say stagnant and ineffective. His book is misunderstood. Even Martin Luther wanted to cut it out of the bible, because he wrongfully believed it advocated a works-based theology. In reality, what James means is that our works are the outward sign of inward faith. Anyone can say they have faith, but our works confirm it. On the other hand, one can use works as a distraction from the vulnerability that comes from faith, like the unyielding villain of the film, Ra's Al Ghul. He's the leader of the League of Shadows, the guild of assassins that trains Bruce. His heart is hard and lacks empathy. As part of Bruce's initiation, Ra's, demands that he execute a prisoner to prove his resolve. For Ra's, words are meaningless. Bruce escapes, but learns that you can become more than yourself if you are devoted to an ideal. That requires *doing*.

Our actions don't just define *us;* they define Christ. The world judges Jesus by his followers. If, like Bruce Wayne training to be Batman, we devote ourselves to Christ's ideals, then our actions will point back to Him as vibrantly as the bat signal. There are times when all we can offer are words; give them. But there are also times when we can take action; do so. Give a buck to a hungry stranger. Help someone fix a flat. Volunteer at a food pantry. And don't fear that it is a waste of time if you don't talk about the gospel; you won't have to say a word about your faith, because you will be too busy showing it.

JOURNAL QUESTIONS
- Does your faith journey emphasize faith or works more?
- Based on your works, would others recognize your faith?

~ 25 ~
MAN OF STEEL

"I'm surrendering to mankind.
There's a difference."

Year: 2013
Distributor: Warner Bros.
Producers: Charles Roven, Christopher Nolan, Emma Thomas, Zack Snyder
Director: Zack Snyder
Writer: David S. Goyer
Runtime: 143 minutes
Rating: PG-13 for intense sequences of sci-fi violence, action and destruction, and for some language

Scripture Reading: Matthew 26:36-56

Today's movie is divisive, to say the least. Following the success of *The Dark Knight* trilogy, *Man of Steel* sought to reboot *Superman* with a more serious interpretation of character's origins. Lauded by fans for its high-octane action and grounded tone, but denounced by others for its wanton destruction as Superman and Zod destroy Metropolis while a device called a World Engine turns it into a new Krypton. Suffice it to say, *Man of Steel* is a lot to unpack.

101

It's easy to draw comparisons to the classic Donner film, but I would rather address this movie based on its own merit than have a point-counterpoint of the two. That said, there are a few details I think should be addressed. First, the differences between the prologues. While Donner's Krypton is cold and icy, Zack Snyder's Krypton is colorful and lively. Both get Kal to Earth following the destruction of Krypton, and both give us glimpses of his upbringing (including the death of his human father, Jonathan Kent, one of this film's controversial choices). Both set up Zod as a villain, as well as the Phantom Zone, and both depict Clark not stepping into his own as Superman until the same age as Jesus at the time of his ministry. The difference is that Donner made him 30 (the start of His ministry) and Snyder made him 33 (the end of His ministry). But neither explains how a man with no past or experience gets a job as a reporter.

References to Jesus become as eclipsing to the film as the World Engine is to Metropolis. Superman stretches out like a cross *twice*, Jor-El's tells him that he's a bridge between two worlds, and he willingly surrenders in spite of his power to evade imprisonment.

As someone whose raison d'etre is drawing spiritual lessons from pop culture, even I find it distracting. One of the reasons that those of us who aren't crazy about this film prefer Reeve as Superman is because Cavill comes across as stiff and emotionless. I don't blame him, he seems to have been encumbered by a directorial mandate to focus more on being *perfect* than being *super*. Perhaps this is why so many hated Superman killing Zod at the end (though he indirectly killed him in *Superman II* and *directly* executed him in the comics); it seemed incongruent with the Jesus metaphor he was presented to be.

As I said in Chapter 1, we aren't suppose to relate to Superman, he is trying to relate to us. It's also one of the reasons why God came down in the person of Jesus. Reeve balanced confidence, humility, and compassion. That said, Cavill better portrays learning how to be human.

Overt as it may be, the scene of Superman letting himself be arrested is powerful and does evoke the image of Gethsemane, where Jesus allowed himself to be detained. It might not seem obvious, but Judas and Zod have parallels too. Both are zealots who viewed their target as the way to see their goals realized. Judas thought the capture of Jesus would be a rallying cry for revolution; Zod also wanted an uprising, by terraforming Earth into a new Krypton using Superman's DNA. Even their deaths mirror one another's.

True, Judas hanged himself and Superman snaps Zod's neck, but how does one die from hanging? If done correctly, the victim's neck it snapped by gravity. The scene is a reference to Genesis 3:15, that the Lord will crush Satan's head.

Superman and Christ are powerful enough to avoid capture; their shackles were symbolic. Superman even admits to Lois Lane that he only let the soldiers put them on him because it made them feel better. Likewise, Jesus reminds the crowd that He could summon legions of angels to His aid.

The two surrendered, not to their persecutors but to their purpose, and each set for us an example of obedience. They both came to serve, and they both stand for Hope, but Superman merely invites us to join him in the sun; he will always fly above us. Jesus, on the other hand, makes us super too, and invites us to join Him in the clouds.

JOURNAL QUESTIONS
- In what areas do you struggle to obey God's will?
- What was the hardest thing God asked you to do? Did you?

~ IN ~
CLOSING

"Until such time as the world ends, we will act as though it intends to spin on."

Nick Fury, *The Avengers* (2012)

When I was a kid, the thought of quality superhero movies like we have now was a pipe dream. Other than the occasional *Batman* sequel, there was little at the box office for superhero fans. My favorite movie was *Superman II* as a boy. I watched it so often that my mom, a typist working from home, had to catch herself from unconsciously writing quotes in her reports. Luckily she caught them, or her boss may have had words with her when he read such choice Zod lines as, "Who is this imbecile," "You will bow down before me," or "Why do say this to me, when you know I will kill you for it?"

I remember seeing *X-Men* for the first time, and, as much as I didn't care for some of the creative choices, it was great to see the characters in action. Years later, when *Spider-*

Man came out, I never dreamed I'd see him onscreen with Captain America and Iron Man in a movie like *Civil War.* I never imagined I'd have enough material to fill a devotional one day. I never thought we would talk about a "Cinematic Universe," or compare one studio's with another's. I don't think anyone did, yet it strikes me that we seem to be more preoccupied with nitpicking what we don't like about these films than we are grateful for having them.

So does that mean *every* superhero film is gold, and Teflon-coated against criticism? Of course not! Take some of the movies in this book, for instance. I was just as frustrated as any fan that the Joker killed Bruce Wayne's parents in the Burton film (once I read enough comics to know why that was wrong, anyway). I hated the Green Goblin costume in *Spider-Man*, and I am *still* waiting for a faithful version of Doctor Doom. There's nothing wrong with criticism, but let us not be so critical that we forget to be grateful for having these movie to criticize in the first place. We aren't going to have it this good forever.

Audiences are fickle. There was a time when westerns were all the rage. Now, we get very few. I could say the same thing about any genre. Sure, superheroes are en vogue today, but once DC exhausts itself in a scramble to catch up with the MCU, and after even the MCU has run its course, then what? Will we crave costumed crusaders in a couple of years as much as we do today? I don't think so. The day is coming (and some predict soon) when appetites will change and the few superhero flicks we get will be a treat, just as we're lucky when we get a new gangster movie or western.

Why am I making such a point about the superhero genre's inevitable wane? Because the same thing will happen to Christianity. 2 Timothy 4:3-4 says "For the time will come when people will not put up with sound doctrine. Instead, to suit their own desires, they will gather around them a great number of teachers to say what their itching ears want to hear. They will turn their ears away from the truth and turn aside to myths." Some believe that time is here, and I'm not sure I disagree. In just the last seven years, there has been an approximate 10% dip in religious affiliation in the US.[1] I don't think that the church will ever cease to exist, but it is receding. Is it a matter of changing tastes, like movie genres, or is there something more nefarious at work?

In superhero movies, citizens turn costumed vigilante to help the overworked legal system deal with the threat of supervillains. The Church has it's fair share of 'villains,' too. Some are secular individuals who intentionally target us, but many come from within the Church itself. Christians can be Christianity's worst enemy. At the very least, those who *use* Christianity to advance political or personal agendas that make the rest of us look bad, or stirs up division.

Just as comics have teams like the Avengers, Justice League, or the X-Men, Christianity has a number of 'teams,' too; denominations, each holding distinct views on how best to practice our faith. Some get along; others do not, and think they are the one, true way. What message do outsiders receive when we fight amongst ourselves? Like Iron Man and Captain America coming to blows in *Civil War*, they learn that being right is more important to us than scriptures that call us to unity.

The Church is hurting. We can armchair quarter-back that like we do when movies get something 'wrong' from the comics, or we can do something about it. Just as heroes rise to help law enforcement in their cities, we must be willing to don cape and cowl to help the Church, because we *are* the Church; it's up to each of us to do our part. We need to stop wasting time fighting each other and get to work, because, as with superhero movies, we won't have it this good forever.

~ NOTES ~

EPIGRAPH

1.) If Christopher Reeve was a hero to you, consider being a hero too and making a donation to the Christopher and Dana Reeve Foundation:
https://www.christopherreeve.org/

INTRODUCTION

1.) Great examination of this in the article below:
http://www.cnbc.com/2014/12/30/why-comic-books-are-big-business.html

2.) Here is an excellent breakdown of sales statistics from over the years. Note the relationship between sales and money. Increased costs have led to higher grosses, but the number of copies sold is where it was 20 years ago.
http://www.comichron.com/yearlycomicssales.html

CHAPTER 3

1.) While there are a number of reprints to choose from, for my money I recommend *Marvel Masterworks: The Amazing Spider-Man* Vol. 1 (ISBN-10:0785191313) by Stan Lee and Steve Ditko. It collects *Amazing Fantasy #15* and the first 10 issues of *The Amazing Spider-Man.*

CHAPTER 4

1.) You can find a number of articles on the bizarre history of the Fantastic Four on film, but there is also a full length documentary about it. Check out info for the movie and where to stream it here:
http://doomedthemovie.com/

CHAPTER 7

1.) Great interview of Peter Laird and Kevin Eastman on creating the Ninja Turtles, including the connections to Daredevil as well as early designs: *http://theweek.com/captured/446321/fascinating-origin-story-teenage-mutant-ninja-turtles*

CHAPTER 12

1.) *The Monster Gospels* (2017) by yours truly. I've included a bonus chapter from the book for you. If you like it, try it out. You don't have to like horror to appreciate the reflections, and there's plenty of plot summary if you don't want to watch the movies we address.

CHAPTER 16

1.) In the time between the first draft and the second draft it went from 4.2 to 4.5. Check it out: *http://www.boxofficemojo.com/franchises/chart/? view=main&id=avengers.htm&sort=opengross&order=DESC &p=.htm*

IN CLOSING

1.) Eye-opening stats concerning the secularization of the nation's non-religious persons can be found here: *http://www.pewresearch.org/fact-tank/2015/11/11/religious-nones-are-not-only-growing-theyre-becoming-more-secular/*

~ A FEW ~
ACKNOWLEDGMENTS

Some of my happiest memories are of Father's Days and birthdays when I got to see many of the movies in this book with my father, **Richard Korsiak**. Thanks for making those memories with me.

My mother, **Diane Korsiak**, is a saint if for no other reason than she indulged me watching some of these movies hundreds of times. Thank you for loving me enough to let me explore my interests.

Thank you, **Kerry Foote**, for seeing my potential and giving me the opportunity to preach about Spider-Man, not just at one church but two.

Thank you once again, **Brian Trumble**, for another great cover, for your help with editing, for the author photo, and for holding the book hostage so that I would go to the doctor when I didn't want to. Also, thank you for reminding me of Plato's cave.

Thanks **Jodie Griggs** and **Austin West** for weathering a tropical storm to see *Batman*. And Austin, thanks for the popcorn.

~ ABOUT ~
THE AUTHOR

When not weaving pithy homilies about superhero movies, Jason Korsiak can be found weaving pithy homilies about horror movies in his book, *The Monster Gospels*, or weaving pithy homilies about holiday specials in his book, *The Christmas Gospels*. He has a variety of other interests, and looks forward to using them as an excuse to binge on movies and weave pithy homilies about them too.

Jason was a Youth Pastor for seven years. During this time, he worked as a Worship Director for three years and as a Contemporary Worship Service Coordinator for five years. Though he believes that he became a Christian when he was 7, Jason did not become involved with church until he was 16-years-old. He volunteered in Youth and Drama ministries for six years before becoming a Youth Pastor professionally and has a BA in Psychology with a Minor in Religion from Saint Leo University, and lives in West-Central Florida with his dog and cat. In his spare time, Jason enjoys illustration, video production, and photography.

A NIGHTMARE ON ELM STREET

"Whatever you do...don't fall asleep."

Year: 1984
Distributor: New Line Cinema
Producer: Robert Shaye
Director: Wes Craven
Writer: Wes Craven
Runtime: 91 minutes
Rating: R

Scripture Reading: Exodus 34:6-7

It's impossible to overstate just how much this film series means to me; not only is Freddy Krueger my favorite monster, but simply one of my favorite fictional characters. Imagine my excitement to learn that actor Robert Englund was making a convention appearance not far from me. It was his first appearance at this con, so the line stretched around the resort for what must have been miles. In fact, we waited three hours to see him.

As my friend and I got closer, I could hear Englund

banter with fans. He seemed to have boundless enthusiasm. Then, at last, he shouted, "Next victim, please!" in signature Freddy fashion. Cautiously, I told him my story.

It was spring of 1988 and Freddy fever was in the air. *Nightmare* posters filled shop windows down the boulevard where I lived in Queens to promote the release of *Part 4: the Dream Master*. Occasionally a curious, non-licensed trinket would pop up on store counters, and gloves and masks were ready for Halloween. One night, my parents watched a VHS of today's film, but unbeknownst to them I had sneaked out of bed and was hiding between their lounge chairs. My five year old mind was filled with awe and terror, inspiring some Freddy nightmares of my own. Like the heroes of the film, I was afraid to go to sleep. It was impossible to escape Freddy in those days. Between the persistent ads everywhere and the dreams I was having, it seemed as though Freddy's reach was as long as his arms in Tina's alley. Terrified as I was of him, I was also fascinated. My parents took a unique approach for getting me over my fear; rather than shielding me, as many other parents would have, they let me watch the movies until I wasn't scared anymore. By demystifying him, Freddy was stripped of his power to frighten me, just like in the movie. My parents then had me watch a behind-the-scenes documentary about the making of *Dream Master,* which not only showed me that Freddy was just an actor in makeup but also how movies are made. This motivated me to make a *Nightmare* movie of my own, a feature-length fan film called *Freddy's Return: A Nightmare Reborn,* which is set between the events of *Nightmare 5* and *Freddy's Dead.*

Englund's gaze was piercing. He praised my parents for being supportive and said that he wished more parents were like them. Some parents, in an effort to protect their children, teach them to be ashamed of themselves because of their interests, instead.

A Nightmare on Elm Street is about the damage that parents can do, even those with the best intentions. Killing a man who got away with murdering their children seemed to be *justified,* but it wasn't *right,* and their "sin" came back to haunt them. Today's scripture celebrates God's compassion but warns that He will punish children, even grandchildren, for the sins of their parents. How can God be compassionate while also punishing innocent children?

When I was a youth pastor, I often said that Youth Ministry meant having one day a week to drive home what home drives out the other six. Children suffer from their parents' poor choices. Too often, those children make similar choices and create a pattern as distinct as Freddy's striped sweater. God does not punish children for the sins of their parents but for sins that they learned from their parents and then commit themselves. This verse is a caution to raise our children well so that they don't make our mistakes.

Nightmare is about children who suffer because of their parents' sins but break the cycle. At first, Nancy wants to bring Freddy into reality so that she can prove her story. Like her parents, her motive is selfish. As she comes to terms with the fact that she can't *manage* Freddy, Nancy does the one thing that can break the impulsive line of thinking that created him: turns her back. In the same way, repentance, which literally means *to turn*, is the only way to break Sin's hold in our lives, but we first have to wake up and recognize it; sin, like Freddy, catches us sleeping.

I am so grateful for my supportive family. Not every child has that blessing. Thankfully, whether our parents were great or not so great, their sins do not have to determine our future; we have the power to turn our back on sin patterns, but that doesn't mean temptation can't arise again. At the end of the movie, the potential for Freddy's return exists, as it does for each of us and our personal "Freddy." Whatever we do, we must not fall back to sleep.

ALSO FROM JASON KORSIAK

THE CHRISTMAS GOSPELS

Can Rudolph help us love ourselves? Can the Grinch teach us how to be a better neighbor? Can Ralphie's air rifle show the meaning of contentment?

All these answers and more are wrapped in the pages of THE CHRISTMAS GOSPELS - 26 spiritual reflections inspired by some of the greatest holiday specials of all time!

ISBN-13: 978-1541090484

ISBN-10: 1541090484

ENJOY THIS BONUS PREVIEW CHAPTER!

~ 10 ~
SANTA CLAUS: THE MOVIE

"If you give extra kisses, you get bigger hugs."

Year: 1985
Distributor: TriStar Pictures
Producers: Pierre Spengler, Ilya Salkind
Director: Jeannot Szwarc
Writer: David Newman
Runtime: 107 minutes
Rating: PG

Scripture Reading: Matthew 25:1-13

Today's film is polarizing. From the director of such "hits" as *Jaws 2* and *Supergirl*, *Santa Claus: The Movie* is a bizarre attempt to interpret Santa's lore with the sensibility of *Superman: The Movie*. Both films even end with a man flying past the earth and looking at the camera. Claus is a toy maker from Scandinavia who nearly freezes to death with his wife on Christmas Eve while delivering gifts. They are rescued by the vendegum, beings who prefer to be called elves and live in an invisible ice world. A fortress of solitude, you might say. They've been preparing for Claus for a long time; a prophecy said a toy maker would come who loved children and would give their gifts to the world. Becoming Santa, Claus montages through the centuries, delivering gifts and building his legend. Santa is moved by a homeless boy named Joe when he arrives in 80's New York. Joe is smitten with a girl named Cornelia who leaves him food. Her step-uncle, B.Z., is an evil CEO who runs a toy company and was modeled after Gene Hackman in *Superman.*

An uppity elf named Patch tries to prove himself as Santa's assistant by building an assembly-line-style machine to create the toys for the year, but it fails and all the gifts break, humiliating Santa. Patch steps down, and the job goes to an elf named Puffy who isn't as *productive* as Patch but strives for excellence. Hoping to regain Santa's favor, Patch leaves and joins B.Z., creating lollipops that make kids float, but all B.Z. sees is a potential fortune, so he convinces Patch to make a more potent formula that he can sell as candy canes which will make children fly.

Joe is caught eavesdropping with Cornelia, and he is taken away, but Cornelia learns that the candy canes explode with heat, so she sends Santa a letter, begging for help. Joe is discovered by Patch, who decides to take him and the candy canes to the North Pole, not knowing that they will explode.

The finale is a race against time as Santa tries to catch Patch and Joe before Patch's magic flying car blows up.

The film earned just $23 million of its $50 million budget back and garnered mostly negative reviews. Still, it's gained a cult following and is one of my favorite Christmas movies. So far as I was concerned, David Huddleston was the real Santa, and I believed in the movie because of the weight it gave everything. With the exception of B.Z., who gobbles up scenery like magic candy canes, everyone takes it seriously. The scene when the Ancient Elf, played by Burgess Meredith, anoints Santa has tremendous power. Scenes like when Patch resigns or when Santa grieves to his wife about it are intensely dramatic; the movie doesn't have a lot of *story*, but it has a whole lot of *heart*.

There's a tender moment early in the film in the Toy Tunnel, an endless warehouse of the toys that the elves made anticipating Santa's arrival. They toiled for centuries because they believed so strongly in the prophecy that Santa would come. I'm reminded of the parable about ten virgins who were told to wait and greet a groom with lanterns. Five wise ones stood watch and had lanterns ready, but the other five were unwise; they not only didn't fill their lanterns with oil but also fell asleep. When the groom arrived, it was too late and they were left out of the wedding. The parable is about Jesus' return. We don't know when He will come back, so we should be shrewd with our time. The elves were like the wise virgins, working with the confidence that their faith would be rewarded.

I got to be an elf once, on my school's float for a Christmas parade when I was in fifth grade. My job was to sit at the front, which was Santa's toy shop, and hammer at toys. I kept forgetting to, though, because, as a fifth grader, I felt like a star and kept waving at the crowd instead. As I think of the elves, working in hope that Santa would come, I wonder how often I'm like the unwise virgins in the parable. We preach that Jesus will come back, but do we live like it? Do we roll up our sleeves and hammer away or do we smile and wave? Then again, some believers are like Patch, way too zealous and doing more harm than good. We find balance being like Puffy, knowing the Christmas Eve deadline will come but working in steady excellence until it does.

JOURNAL QUESTIONS
- How can a competitive spirit get in the way of Christmas?
- How can we live in the present and be mindful of the fact we have an unknown spiritual "deadline?"

Made in the USA
Columbia, SC
19 November 2017